BAD Christmas

Funny Stories about terrible Christmases

Editor   Mike Jackson

Cartoons   Adey Bryant
Design   Lisa Griffiths

Severnpix

First published by Severnpix September 2005

Copyright © Mike Jackson 2005

A catalogue record for this book is available from the British Library

ISBN 0-9545402-5-5

Printed and bound in Great Britain by HSW Print, Tonypandy.

WHAT DO YOU MEAN -
BAD CHRISTMAS?

How can it be bad? It's a holiday, isn't it? And you get presents. And you eat turkey. And you drink lots of alcohol - if you're over eleven.

So what could be bad about it?

Well, plenty.

The good Christmas is where we all have a fab family. The Mums are wonderfully talented in the present-picking, wrapping and meal-preparing departments. The Dads are great at dressing up as Santa and amusing the kids with wonderful games. The kids are charming, gracious and totally delighted with their gifts. And the relations are all welcomed guests adding merriment, wit and generosity to the party atmosphere.

So when did you last have a Christmas like that?

Never? Then join the club.

Our first Christmas in this house was spent squeezing the catering foil for the turkey into crevices below the kitchen cupboards after my wife spotted a mouse scuttling underneath the cooker on Christmas Eve. We had moved in to the badly converted barn only a few days earlier and were starting to discover why we'd got the place so cheap. Our Christmas lunch was a Cup-a-Soup. The turkey stayed in the fridge until Rentokil were able to visit – mid January.

Last year Gil tackled a Delia non-meat special, but spilled parsnip sauce on the floor, then slipped in it and fell over and sprained her ankle, so we abandoned the squashed roulade and headed off in a hurry to the Worcester A&E where we spent the rest of the special day in the glum company of those who had cut themselves open, tripped over cables, fallen off bikes, or in some other way gone beyond the bounds of sensible health and safety practice.

Consuming the remnants of the foyer crisp and chocolate vending machines made Cup-a-Soup seem distinctly seasonal. Were we complaining? Of course not, because most of the other folk around us had unquestionably worse symptoms.

Yes, everyone there was experiencing a Bad Christmas, but I have discovered that you don't need to go near a hospital to feel the season is a terrible time – expensive, troublesome, contrived and capable of reminding you all too vividly of how far removed your life is from those idealised versions portrayed on TV where beautiful people partake of fancy fondants and liqueurs, in front of an exquisitely dressed tree shored up with glorious presents.

Yeah, we hate all that. Because it's far removed from the grim truth. And anyway, doesn't the whole thing stink – wasting time, money, and the globe's increasingly precious resources.

Scrooge said: *"If I could work my will every idiot who goes about with a 'Merry Christmas' on his lips should be boiled with his own pudding, and buried with a stake of holly through his heart."*

Well, that's a bit extreme, but, in these days of abundance and indulgence, we say: No shame in Scrooginess. Cut the contrivances, abandon the elaborate, expel the excess. Return, perhaps, to a Dickensian simplicity, dignity and worth.

Within these pages you can relish in the awfulness of the contemporary event. And know that you are not alone in having ghastly memories of the whole occasion.

We've gathered together horror stories about this special time of the year. Accidents and anomalies, downsides and disasters, mistakes and miseries, troubles and even a few tragedies.

We've also poked our heads into a range of regional and national newspapers and magazines to review the values, issues, incidents and journalism applied to the season of goodwill.

(Our thanks to everyone who submitted first person or third person anecdotes and observations, and to journalists and media organisations who gave us permission to draw on their work. Where requested, and as appropriate, we have changed names, places and references to ensure the anonymity of certain parties.)

Let's face it, reading this will make you feel better about the whole damn Christmas thing. And help you see it through, and out the other end - when life can get back to something like normal.

Mike Jackson, Worcestershire

CONTENTS

"I need a new outfit for the office party."

BAD DEEDS

You're stretching up on the chair to put the fairy on top of the tree.
One more little push, and suddenly you and the tree and the chair are in one big heap on the carpet, and the baby is biting into a glass bauble.
Typical stuff, according to the Royal Society for the Prevention of Accidents.
They estimate 80,000 people attend hospital over the 12 twelve days of the holidays having had a mishap in or around the house.
While Dad's poking his eye out on pine needles, Mum's pouring turkey fat down her chest having let the roasting dish tip up.
6,000 people ended up in A&E on Christmas Day itself.
Top causes were: tripping over cables connecting new electrical goods to plug sockets, stabbing oneself or someone else with scissors whilst opening presents, and falling down the stairs after a drunken visit to the toilet.
But there are a hundred and one ways for Christmas to go wrong . . .

ROCKET BOY
My husband and I had a few drinks on Christmas Eve and so didn't hear our four year old George get up. Whether he came in to see us we'll never know, but when we awoke we could hear him downstairs. I leapt up and ran down to find him in the living room surrounded by wrapping paper and all sorts of presents, not just children's things.
He'd opened everything under the Christmas tree, including my sister's idea of a joke for me – a vibrator, which George was swinging through the air, having decided it was a space rocket.
He wouldn't be parted from it, so, before the rest of the family arrived, my husband disguised it by felt-tip penning port-holes and a door on the side, and sticking some red crepe paper on the base to look like flames coming out of the engine.
I think we got away with it, because no-one made any comments about the bizarre toy that flew around the house on Christmas Day – though I drew the line at it hovering over the turkey on the dining table.

Mary Meacham, Harrogate

TEAR OFF A STRIP
Why is it that so many charities think the way to advance their cause is to produce a calendar with a number of their supporters in a state of undress?
Our local paper was plastered with pictures of teenage girls in their underwear raising money for young people suffering from cancer.
Where had they taken the pictures? In the local pub.
In fact the landlord joined in himself, taking his shirt off so he could pose in the midst of the semi-naked girls with his arms round a couple of them.
He certainly looked like he was enjoying himself, surrounded by a bobbing sea of red bras.
Surely there are better ways of doing charitable work?

Marjorie Wishbold, Nottingham

CARD CHECK
My ex-wife was distinctly anal over Christmas cards. She kept meticulous records of what she sent and received, including dates.
If she didn't get a card from someone, she would post them what amounted to a questionnaire, along the lines of: "Happy New Year. We were surprised not to receive a card from you. Was this because it got lost in the post, or you

didn't send one? Have you been too busy, ill, or do you consider an exchange of cards with us is not appropriate" etc.

I dissuaded her from including a stamped addressed envelope.

Barry, Bristol

KEEP THEM UNDER WRAPS

My son Matthew went to a playgroup that announced a special animal Christmas party for all its youngsters. Matthew's a bit nervous about animals and so I spoke to one of the supervisors who assured me there would be nothing to worry about – just a few bunny rabbits kept under control.

When I collected him after the party I could see straightaway he was upset. He howled when he got home and told me a giant spider had attacked him.

It turned out the animal handlers brought snakes and a tarantula but kept them in their van until the children nagged them into bringing them in.

Matthew suffered nightmares for weeks.

Paula Hildred, Eastbourne

NOT SO PRETTY POLLY

'Parrot saves family' was the headline after Charlie the parrot raised the alarm in a house in Durham when the Christmas lights set the tree on fire. Everyone escaped from the property, thanks to the bird's ability to squawk.

You can be sure they treated the pet with kindness after that sobering emergency.

Well, they would have done, but unfortunately they had left Charlie behind, and he went up in smoke.

DRIVE YOU MAD

How about this for a Christmas present – I bought my girlfriend a second-hand but very good condition convertible VW Beetle. I kept it at a friend's house for a couple of days then drove it to our place on Christmas Eve.

Alice was in the kitchen and we had no plans to go out that night, so I just had to make sure she didn't look out the front window for the rest of the evening.

My plan was to get up very early in the morning and cover the car in wrapping paper, then show it to her.

I took a last peep at it before going to bed and was dead chuffed at my generosity, and successful plans to give her this massive Christmas surprise.

I woke up about half past six on Christmas morning. Alice was still asleep. I got up and went downstairs and opened the front door to see an empty drive. The car had been stolen in the night.

Needless to say I was gutted.

Alice took it very well. It was some time before she was convinced that I really had bought her a car and that it had been nicked, but I was so furious all morning she concluded that I wasn't just putting it on.

The police came round in the afternoon and took the details.

Then on Boxing Day they rang to say another force had found it – burnt out. I wanted to take Alice to see the wreck, but she didn't want to go.

Bill Field, Cheshire

NO KILLJOY

Fathers slumped in doorways lying in their own vomit, youths fighting in pubs with Santa hats still on their heads. Kids begging at your door singing badly-worded carols, a menacing grin as you dip into your pension. Even TV has lost its shine since they took Noel Edmonds off air.

Shandy Davenport, Gloucester

GOING NOWHERE

As a novelty for my family during the holidays, I booked tickets for a steam railway trip from Wolverhampton to Carlisle.

We arrived at Codsall station at half six in the morning. It was freezing cold, but we were in good time for the train that was due to arrive at 6.45.

By seven there was still no sign of it, and no station staff available to tell us how long we'd have to wait.

There's no proper waiting room, and nowhere to get a hot drink, so we were pretty miserable.

Having paid out over £100, we hung on in hope, along with dozens of others. It was 8 o'clock before someone managed to speak to one of the tour managers in Liverpool who told them the trip was cancelled because they couldn't get the heater working on the train so it was still in the sidings.

Would have been nice if they'd sent someone to tell us first thing, instead of us being left to freeze half to death.

Ann Meads, Pendeford

A MONTH TO GO

December is a very special month.

In Britain, it's the most popular month for shopping, killing turkeys and one's fellow human beings.

Yes, statistically you're more likely to be murdered, or to murder, for that matter, during the season of goodwill.

TAKING ACCOUNT

I'm a new business manager for a branch of a High Street bank.

A week before Christmas a man made an appointment to see me. He told me he used another bank up the road and had become very unhappy with their treatment of him. I listened to his experiences and assured him that we would try to offer him a better service.

Our central heating was up high, and it was very warm in the customer office. We both took our jackets off and hung them over our chairs.

I typed his details into our computer system. He seemed very uneasy about this and muttered a lot about his changing circumstances. This isn't unusual if someone's marriage is breaking up, but this fellow was unusually edgy.

He told me he wanted to look at the paperwork before he proceeded. Then he said he would like a copy of what I had put into our system. I went off to get this from the printer and when I returned, the man had gone, along with my wallet, that he'd lifted out of my jacket pocket, and which had £50 in cash inside, that I was going to use to buy some Christmas presents that lunchtime.

Our competitors up the road had never heard of him.

Wallace Hewlett, Southampton

BIT OF BAD LUCK

You're a drug dealer conducting an illicit "narcotics transaction" in a fast food restaurant car park late one evening. All is going according to plan, until a police patrol vehicle cruises by and the officers inside suspect you're up to no good.

Time for a quick getaway. You roar off at 100 miles an hour. The police car is in pursuit, but the cops aren't close enough to read your number plate.

You take a right and bang into another car but you keep going. The police stop to attend to the other motorist. You've got away with it.

You patch up your car and look forward to Christmas a week later. But on the special day a fight breaks out at home and your other half calls the cops.

They turn up and try to settle the domestic dispute. Then they notice your vehicle on the drive.

They spot the dents on the side, the paint job you undertook (using the wrong colour paint), the missing bits of trim, the broken mirror – all in the areas where your automobile hit the other one in the midst of your successful getaway.

They've got you.

That's Christmas for you.

SILENT NIGHT

To kill time one evening I agreed to go along on a carol singing trip around the houses in our village.

One of the other carol singers was a very attractive woman who seemed to immediately take a fancy to me. As we worked our way from house to house we started to chat and flirt. After a few mince pies and sherries, we really had the hots for each other.

At one house Penelope asked if she could use the bathroom. The owners told her it was at the top of the stairs. She went up there, and so I nipped up a few seconds later. When she opened the bathroom door, I grabbed her and starting kissing her passionately. We both went back into the bathroom and locked the door.

The leader of the choir group came up and knocked. I told him I'd catch him up and that Penelope had gone outside to get some fresh air.

So our fellow choristers carried on to the next house, whilst we made love in the bathroom. Five minutes later we came down the stairs, Penelope pretending she had felt ill, and me pretending I was looking after her.

The couple gave us a very dirty look. I always wonder if they figured out the truth.

Edward, Ealing

TOSSER

An American teenager on Christmas Eve was arraigned on a series of serious charges: first-degree assault, first degree reckless endangerment, criminal mischief, possession of stolen property and forgery.

How had that all come about?

He had used a stolen credit card with fake identification to buy a turkey. The butcher became suspicious and called the cops, who trailed the youth as he drove away from the shop.

The thief saw the police car and so tossed the turkey out of the window. It bounced on to the bonnet of another car and went through the windscreen seriously injuring the driver.

SPECIAL DAY

A young Mum near us got into a lot of trouble for having gone off to Spain to see a football match with her boyfriend, leaving her two children alone in their flat.

It was in all the papers when social services found out.

She came back and was charged.

The judge sentenced her to a six month prison sentence, presumably to set an example.

I can't see how this would make life better for her kids, who were put into care. I wonder what sort of Christmas the judge had?

Jackie Thornbury, Birmingham

STAY ON THE DRIVE

Statistically the worst day of the year to be motoring is the 15th December. This is when most accidents occur, according to an analysis by LloydsTSB Insurance.

Shopping tempers fraying, children's last day of chauffeuring to and from school, office party leavers failing to take the taxi option.

December's the worst month for driving, prang-wise, but the 15th stands out in front for kissing goodbye to your no claims bonus.

NICKED MY BALL?

For months I'd been trying to persuade my girlfriend to have oral sex with me. She eventually agreed in principle that we'd do this at Christmas. Then she announced a stipulation – that we would shave our pubes in advance.

This was fine by me.

Next day she came out of the bathroom, and announced she'd done hers. Now it was my turn.

I don't know if you've tried it, but it's not easy. The nature of our testicles is nothing like a man's chin, and it's hard to get a razor to run smoothly along the necessary parts.

I had a stab at it, so to speak, but it wasn't satisfactory, and the whole process was starting to make me feel queasy, so I asked her if she would help me with it.

I think she decided I was a pervert. She blasted a mountain of shaving foam on to my private parts and started to brutally scrape the razor across the hairy areas. Surprise, surprise, she cut me and I passed out at the sight of the blood.

We never did have oral sex.

Malcolm, Fulham

"I swear I'm going to kill my ex-husband!"

11

A TIME FOR SHOPPING

2004 was a Bad Christmas for the retail trade.

Consumer spending was a whole 1% down on December 2003.

Now one miserable little per cent doesn't seem much, but that was the lowest level of pre-Christmas shopping for 20 years.

Could this have been the turning point for the consumer society?

Don't think so.

Brits are more inclined to spend, spend, spend at Christmas than almost any other nation. On average we hurl around a thousand pounds into the tills during December.

Are we spending it wisely?

What do you think?

COLOUR BLIND

I decided to treat myself to a flat screen TV for Christmas, even though I know they don't make the programmes any better.

I brought it home and set it up on Christmas Eve. After using a little portable for years, the picture was fantastic.

My girlfriend had bought some cheap candles from the market, and she insisted on sticking one on top of the new TV, much against my wishes.

She lit the wick and it started to burn more like a dodgy firework than a candle, churning out flames and smoke, and quickly melting the wax, some of which dripped down into the back of the screen.

Goodness knows what happened inside, but some part of the colour processing electronics were damaged, which meant all the Christmas programmes were tinged red.

Mick Davies, Cwmbran

KILL YOUR KIDS THIS CHRISTMAS

Stourport trading standards officers were out in force in the pre-Christmas period, policing shops where dodgy novelty pens were on sale.

The instruments had a latex insect or reptile wrapped round them, hence the name: Creepy-Crawly Pens.

Mm, sounds a delightful stocking filler, doesn't it!

Only snag was - the latex sheaths were slipping off and in danger of choking children.

Swallowing insects?

That'd just be copying what celebrities do on ITV.

SEX SAVES SHOPPING

You're the Mayor of a small market town that has seen its High Street suffer since your predecessors allowed those big supermarkets to open out on the ring road.

How can you help boost business in the centre of town in that critical pre-Christmas period?

By attending the champagne opening of a fresh enterprise.

But what if that new addition is a sex emporium?

That didn't bother Councillor Andrew Dyke of Evesham. He was down there, official chain round his collar and glass of bubbly in his hand to celebrate the launch of Adam and Eve, selling adult toys, DVDs and fetish gifts.

Behind Adam and Eve were Stuart and Katie Gilbert, convinced they could satisfy a gap in the market.

Not everyone was enthusiastic. One woman entered the premises, took a quick glance at the PVC nurses' outfits and yelled "*Degenerate!*"

The local paper phoned the Reverend Edward Pillar - a pillar of Evesham society - for his opinion. Despite not knowing of the business and not wishing to visit it, he honourably e-mailed an observation: "*I do not think that this type of shop is helpful at a time of general moral decline, and will simply feed a sordid fascination with sexuality rather than promoting a healthy attitude towards a beautiful gift given by a generous God.*"

Well, he was right. By the end of January, the Gilberts were declaring their first month of trading as "*astounding, fantastic*". They wouldn't tell us what was their best selling line, but they patently had managed to satisfy Evesham's sordid fascination with sexuality.

CARE AND ATTENTION
My brother Dillion and I spend a challenging day at the mall buying all the items that our elderly mother had said she needed for her Christmas shopping and cooking.

We were very pleased with ourselves that we'd managed to find everything and had just started back when a drunk stepped off the sidewalk right in front of our car.

Dillon braked hard, but bumped into the guy, who collapsed on the road in front of us.

Mercifully the fellow was okay. Just bruised.

We took him back to his apartment and stayed there for a couple of hours to be absolutely sure he was okay, then we headed back to mother's – and got a severe reprimand for being so late.

We never told her the reason.

Mabel Aslam, Kentucky

BAD FORM
When I told my son Kevin that we were going to see Santa Claus in a department store the following day, he asked if Santa would have an Argos catalogue, and, if not, should he take one.

Cheryl Kelly, Warrington

PARK AND DARK
We went to do our Christmas shopping in Wolverhampton, using the Park and Ride service at Tettenhall. I was worried all day about us getting back to the car park in time. A sign at the bus stop said the gates would shut at six.

We got a bus back which delivered us to the site at 5.15, and the place was closed. The bus driver dropped us off and apologised. We, and half a dozen others, had to hang around for an hour before the fire brigade turned up and cut through the gates so we could retrieve our cars.

Jack Henshaw, Bridgnorth

PRESSING ALL THE WRONG BUTTONS
If you're toying with buying one of the kids a computer game for Christmas, we recommend you study the reviews penned by Neil McGreevy in the Brecon and Radnor Express. He gets to the bottom of their appeal.

'Mortal Kombat Deception': "*The creators have pushed their blood-soaked envelope for spine-removing gore. But when you bore of spilling the claret, why not Kombat chess? Although getting your average Mortal Kombat fan to indulge in chess is a bit like forcing Stephen Hawking to play beach volleyball.*"

'Leisure Suit Larry': *"A puerile adventure that's as filthy as a Frenchman, involving chatting up fantastically breasted women, strip trampolining or guiding Larry's sperm around obstacles."*

GOOD READ?

You're living proof that people like books for Christmas.

Of course over the years there have been lots of books dedicated to the subject of Christmas - though perhaps not many as unimpressed by the season as this.

An early hit was Chapman and Hall's compendium of stories by Charles Dickens in 1907.

Doubtless Alan Titchmarsh's collection of cuddly stuff will blossom, and make our little effort look a miserable weed.

But we reckon 'Bad Christmas' stands a better chance of being read than Bridget Albano's admirable 1995 title: 'Creating Christmas Ornaments from Polymer Clay' - still available on Amazon.

IT'S IN THE WAREHOUSE

Modern phenomenon: Man in white van can only be in several places at once.

People who thought a short cut to Christmas shopping was a few clicks on the internet suffered a growing sense of disappointment as Christmas Eve arrived and the goods they'd paid for failed to turn up.

Whilst Royal Mail managed to get almost everything where it belonged in time, some small firms handling web-based distributors were a bit hit and miss in their deliveries (and that was assuming warehouse staff had been able to find the goods required and package them up).

An estimated half a million people ordered a Christmas present over the internet which failed to arrive in time.

LAP IT UP

Devilishly clever those Japanese businessmen. They can identify people's needs, then satisfy them.

What's one of the nicest things about women? Why, their laps, of course.

So good to rest your head against – if they'll let you.

So a Tokyo firm manufactured artificial laps as Christmas presents – a sort of pillow in a mini-skirt. The items became one of the best-sellers across the country, and not just in sex shops.

WISE MAN?

How can you combine religion with shopping? Impossible, say many men of the church. Those two activities are diametrically opposed.

But over Christmas in Accrington consumers encountered an "if you can't beat them, join them" prospect, when an Asda supermarket temporarily hired Bishop Philip Rushton to stack shelves, and talk to shoppers about Christianity.

But he didn't work there on Sundays, when athiests could meander along the aisles in peace.

YOU NEED RETAIL THERAPY?

You've stocked the shop with all the Christmas stuff any customer might need. And it's December, and business is slow.

So when's it going to pick up?

Well, day by day, there's a bit more interest, but come the middle of the month you're starting to think you might have ordered too much.

It gets to the third week, and you're examining your returns policy with suppliers. What goods can you give back without having to pay for them?

It gets to the fourth week, and still the bastards… sorry, the charming locals who warmly patronise your premises… aren't parting with their cash.

Bugger this for game, I'm going to sell up in the New Year, you're saying to yourself behind that under-utilised till.

Then the 23rd of December arrives, and suddenly you're busy. It's your best day of trading. And tomorrow's Christmas Eve. Between 12 noon and 2 pm on Christmas Eve, you have your busiest hour. Thank goodness for that. Then, as a bonus, at 7 minutes past 2 on the afternoon of Christmas Eve, your credit card transactions reach their peak.

After which it starts to die down again.

And you wonder: Shall I do it all again next year?

BREEDING LIKE BUNNIES

Which chain store had a record Christmas across its 120 branches? Why Ann Summers, whose best selling line was a vibrator called Rampant Rabbit, closely followed by toffee body drizzle. Don't ask!

OUCH

For years I've been very unhappy about my shape, and so I asked my husband and parents if they would pay for me to have some cosmetic surgery as a Christmas present.

They agreed, and so in November I had a series of operations to improve my hips and boobs.

It was agony. I was sore and stiff for weeks on end – right through Christmas, in fact.

In the mirror I can hardly see any difference in myself, and I now feel I stupidly wasted thousands of pounds of my family's cash.

Kelly, Banbury

JESUS WEPT

If Christ can see us now, 2,000 years on from his brief time on earth, what must he make of it?

A quarter of the globe is full of people with more money than sense, whilst the rest are struggling to find food for their children. The rich ride out of their machine-packed palaces to collect more possessions, and on other parts of the planet, families forage on rubbish heaps for fragments of shelter.

Allegedly to acknowledge his birth, the supremely comfortable indulge in an absurd accumulation and exchange of even more objects, none of which they need.

I can't believe he would approve.

Heather Montaque, Derbyshire

ROAD TRAFFIC INCIDENT?

My wife wanted some bookcases to tidy up our books before our visitors came for Christmas.

I was sent off to Focus DoItAll to acquire sufficient units to take our big collection that had occupied the living room floor for far too long.

In the store I found a type of unit that seemed right for the job. One example was on display, and they had two in boxes. I needed three sets, so they agreed that I could have the display model as well as the flat-pack versions.

Unfortunately their trolleys are designed to carry items in boxes, but not five foot high assembled bookshelves.

I got the two flatpacks out to the car and was aware it was now extremely windy. I went back for the display unit that I had to stand up vertically on the trolley to get out of the building.

I started to push it carefully across the car park, where the wind was now gusting quite ferociously. Suddenly a gust caught the bookcase and lifted it off the trolley right on to the bonnet of a parked car with a family sitting inside it. The bookcase crashed across their bonnet, denting it and scratching it.

I had to pay them nearly £400 for repairs to their car, which made it a very expensive set of bookcases.

William Burleigh, Malvern

"I see Alan's got his Christmas face on."

THOSE DAMNED LIGHTS

Are you a SLOTH? A Seasonal Lights On The House fan?
It's a tough one, isn't it.
Does it make people happy or mad?
Is it the best use of electricity or the worst?
Do you or don't you get the drill out and drive some holes into your walls?
Will people admire your efforts or think you're a berk?
But it amuses kids, encourages charity giving – so it must be good.
The SLOTH debate raged through the pages of the regional press during December.
No shortage of views in evidence, not to mention a hundred and one naff plastic Santas doing all sorts of unlikely things half way up gable ends.
Tales of triumph and tragedy, determination and defeat…

CUPPA?

We get on well with our neighbours – for 11 months of the year. But we don't see eye to eye about elaborate illuminated displays pulsating across the road from us in the weeks around Christmas. It's so vulgar.

Our neighbours know our views. They told us they couldn't get their kettle to boil one night because so much power was being used by the flashing tableaux. We told them that if our kettle stopped functioning, we'd come over and rip a few of their luminous Santas off their walls.

Martha Pinton, Leicester

NICKED

Retired market gardener Robert Edwards has become a king of SLOTH.
Ten years ago he began acquiring and displaying lights and novelties in and around his bungalow. So far he's spent £4,000 on equipment, which, once powered up, adds £250 to his electricity bill. He starts the assembly process early November – up the ladders in wind and rain – ready for Switch On.
New elements are hung up weekly to maintain novelty value. And replacing duff lamps is a constant challenge – so many different fittings and voltages.
He has a huge tree at the edge of his property on top of which he manages to mount a giant throbbing electric snowflake.
Hearing children and the elderly appreciate his efforts "*makes my Christmas*", he told us.
Just one snag. His home is on a sharp bend on a busy country road. Motorists roar round the corner to be faced with what looks like a hovering flying saucer, underneath which may be a coach of old folk gazing at Robert's nodding reindeer on the lawn.
The police deployed 'Slow Down' signs on the roads, but they were stolen.
One man knocked on the Edwards's back door to complain and was mesmerised by an animated bull mounting a cow on the kitchen wall.

SHINING IN THE WIND

How many wind turbines would be required to supply the electricity for all the Christmas decorations displayed on the outside of houses this year?

Jenny Haynes, Barton-on-Humber

PLANE DAFT

What's the connection between Concorde and Christmas?

No, we can't think of one either.

So why on earth did a couple of Bristolians build a massive model of the aircraft out of scaffolding poles, plastic sheeting and wire mesh, and stick it in their front garden?

Because they could then load it down with Christmas lights and make it the centre-piece of their seasonal garden display.

Next door the neighbours constructed an 8 feet high version of the Clifton Suspension Bridge.

Now that's obviously got Christmas connections.

Or, maybe not.

IN THE DARK

We made a big effort with our Christmas lights and were short-listed by the local paper as in the top ten attractions. We live on a housing estate with a one-way road system, and lots of cars were struggling to find our place in the evenings, so we put up some signs on lamp-posts, which worked really well. Then guess what? A woman from the council planning department came round and told us we had to take all the signs down.

Talk about the spirit of Christmas.

Sheila Gellard, Swindon

DARK DAYS OF THE POISONED PEN

You work with children with learning difficulties and decide to move to a modest bungalow in a new village. The property needs some attention, and in the months before Christmas you replace some windows and tidy up the overgrown garden. Then, for your grand-children and other visitors, you put up a single string of Christmas lights across the front of the building. Two days later you receive an anonymous letter in the post: "*We would like to welcome you to our village. Perhaps you have noticed since moving here that we foster and enjoy a high level of civic pride in our homes. Unfortunately your dull, ugly front garden and tacky, tawdry lights fail to reflect our village image. Please do what you can to help improve matters. Thank you.*"

You tell the local paper and get lots of sympathetic coverage, including letters of apology from several neighbours, but six months later the author of this poisonous correspondence had still not owned up.

Obviously civic pride getting in the way.

TIME TO LIGHT UP?

If you're going to do that Christmas lights thing all over the front of your house, when should you start?

Well, planning pays dividends.

Toby McLurg of Llandrindod Wells was deploying his first lights on the exterior walls in the second week of November.

Whilst Kevin and Nicola White bought an inflatable tree with two snowmen in a January sale to add to their next display.

Turns out the McLurgs and Whites are next-door-neighbours.

Is this a keeping-up-with-the-Jones's syndrome?

No, they're a team, reflecting in each other's glory by plastering their adjoining premises with electric decorations.

Nicola told us that some of the items consigned to the attic in January don't work when you dig them out again. A Manchester warehouse was having new stock in August, and both families were planning on heading over to alight on the latest models.

DULL

A man from Hazel Grove, Stockport, complained that the council had not put up a Christmas tree in his district.

In response, he was told four sets of fairy lights had been hung on real trees, and over forty illuminated decorations had been erected, but the majority of the relevant budget had already been spent on a memorial garden.

LIGHTEN UP

Perhaps the most touching evidence of neighbourly warmth, bonding, seasonal insanity and grim single-mindedness is the case of Phil Shellam, a seventh-year SLOTH from Gloucester. Each year Phil has dug out his growing collection of flashing reindeer, glowing bells, and glistening snowmen and deployed them artistically around his home.

"We don't just nail them to the wall all higgledy-piggledy, but plan the design on paper months ahead of the launch date."

Alas this year Phil became seriously ill and ended up wheel-chair bound.

So there was no way he could mount those ladders with flashing elves and Lapland railway trains.

Would passers-by be denied their blast of blazing grotto tableaux? Would Phil's box-loads of electrical ephemera from the Far East have to remain in his attic? It seemed that way, until neighbour Mike Meadows stepped in and did on the ladder what circumstances now denied their owner.

Taking instructions from the man below, Mike climbed the walls, hammer, nails and cable in hand, and positioned the synthetic scenery across the brickwork.

Phil told us: *"It made the children's faces light up."*

Who said: *"And half the street!"*

NO GETTING AWAY

If you prefer not to be aware of Christmas for at least a couple of months of the year, avoid driving down the Rhondda valley towards Treherbert, because, on their gable end, right at the side of the main road, Mr and Mrs Price have put up a permanent Christmas lights display.

He's an engineer, and so did a solid job last year, with the intention that the Santas on sledges will never come down.

The good news is that Mrs Price assured us the lights would not be switched on until the 12th of December.

UP TO THE HILT

I borrowed a mate's Hilti nail gun to fix our exterior Christmas lights and a couple of electrical novelties on to the front of our house.

I'd never used one before and didn't know how strong they were.

The first staple fired right through the plastic snowman, cracking it, and causing me to drop it.

Another staple went into my finger, and I fell off the ladder and on to the roof of my car, which thankfully broke my fall.

I gave up after that, but it certainly amused our kids far more than any lights display might have done.

Mark Waverley, Sheffield

SPOILING THE FUN

The Royal Society for the Prevention of Accidents teamed up with the TUC to issue warnings to employees about the dangers of office parties. The effects of alcohol are obviously top of the list, but not far behind, and not unconnected, is dancing on the desk. You might fall off and break a limb, and who's fault would that be? Yours? Or the firm's - for putting the desk there in the first place? Nibbles might result in food poisoning. Mistletoe berries could drop into your twizzlers and make you sick. Sitting naked on the photocopier to reproduce your private parts could result in the glass breaking and your organs becoming speared with splinters.

Oh yes, and sexual activity with other office staff could lead to embarrassment, reduced chances of promotion (depending on who did what to whom, with others finding out or not), sexual disease or pregnancy.

Maybe best to stay at home.

IS THIS A RECORD?

As Christmas presents for my friends I made up individual discs with what I reckoned were their favourite tunes, which I collected off the internet.

Then a week before Christmas we got a solicitors' letter saying we owed the British Phonographic Industry £2,521.36 for down-loading music.

That means my eight Christmas presents cost £315.17 each.

Tanya Evans, Cardiff

CHRISTMAS BOX

A Yorkshire postman decided to knock on people's doors whilst making his last delivery before Christmas, to personally hand over the cards and at the same time wish his customers the compliments of the season. No ulterior motive, but he'd collected more than £50 in tips before one man punched him.

A BIT MICKEY MOUSE

The traditional Christmas California-style includes the heart-warming ceremony of Santa Claus parachuting into the middle of a shopping mall in Anaheim. Em, it's about an old man, presents and TV marketing photo-opportunities.

But guess what, those lovers of fun at Disneyland down the road were worried aircraft in the vicinity of their theme park might spell impending terrorism, and so lobbied successfully for Santa to be grounded.

Father Christmas and the mall marketing team didn't take this lying down. They got a hot air balloon, so Santa could hang around in the sky a hundred feet above the shoppers.

Well, at least it kept the jaundiced juniors at bay.

DOUBLE SPEED

I got a nice Christmas present from Worcestershire Constabulary – two speeding fines – at four minute intervals.

There's a maddening one-way system round the west side of Worcester to control traffic for the cricket ground. I was late for a visit to friends on Christmas Day and took the wrong lane, which meant I had to go right round the one-way system again, and both times I went past a speed camera and got clocked. Wouldn't you have thought they could stand them down on Christmas Day? No way.

Edward Beverley, Birmingham

STEADY AS YOU GO

Metropolitan Police Commissioner Sir John Stevens helpfully laid down some ground rules for the lads' behaviour at the seasonal celebrations: No fighting, no racism remarks, no sexist jokes, and no groping.

Who said the boys couldn't wait for the mistletoe to come down, so things could get back to normal?

FELLED

We were heading home from doing our Christmas shopping when a big Christmas tree fell off the roof rack of the car in front, and bounced on the road, smashed into my front grille, then crashed against my windscreen.

The driver of the car ahead didn't stop.

Our insurers told us that the people in that vehicle probably made an instant decision that it was better to lose a £10 tree than a No Claims Bonus.

Peter Macintosh, Penrith

WRONG AGAIN

A couple of days before Christmas I met an old mate for a drink at a pub in Edgbaston, Birmingham - the Dirty Duck.

He and I were both middle-aged and divorced, resigned to our single state, but always hopeful that things might look up one day on the romantic front.

We had a couple of pints and chewed the fat, observing lots of younger people having fun at other tables.

Imagine our surprise when at the end of the evening some girls asked us if we'd like to come to a party – they were short of men.

We couldn't believe our luck. They said they lived in the next street on the right, off the main road. The door would be open; come along and bring a bottle.

They headed off and we bought a bottle of wine each across the bar, then we got in my car and drove along the main road, then into the first turn on the right. Halfway down was a front door open. We parked and approached the front drive. It was quiet, but we assumed the girls just hadn't got round to putting music on yet.

So we walked into the house and past the staircase and into the kitchen – where there was a woman in her dressing gown rinsing out milk bottles.

She screamed on seeing us and her husband came running down the stairs demanding to know what was going on.

We explained our mistake, apologised and left.

We walked down the street, feeling very foolish, then reached a house from where we could hear music, and that had lots of cars parked outside.

We realised this was the place, even though the door wasn't open.

We rang the bell and an Asian man opened the door. We held up our bottles and said the girls in the pub had invited us. He smiled and ushered us in. The house was packed, with music playing and lots of happy chattering groups of people enjoying tasty-looking food. We moved into the busy living room where couples were dancing.

We were looking round for a corkscrew when it started to dawn on us that we were the only non-Asians in the house.

The host came up. He seemed like a doctor. He politely but firmly ushered us out into the street.

We never did find those girls.

Terry Bartlett, Bromsgrove

SHORT ON GOODWILL

The Chief Executive of Powys County Council decided to use his pre-Christmas message to his team not as a seasonal back-slapping celebration of their achievements over the past year, but to highlight shortcomings. Why were they getting through 57,000 sheets of A4 paper each week? How come they'd spent £238,000 on postage in the last 12 months? Customer service was "dreadful", and how could they have 26 priorities? They needed to prioritise their priorities.

So, no Santa there then.

WEE PROBLEM

An elderly nutty lady in Basildon denied herself any Christmas cheer from the postman when she got it into her head to hurl urine from her potty at anyone who stepped on to her drive.

A spokesman said: *"Dogs we are used to dealing with, but this fell far beyond the bounds of reasonable expectation, and we have not been trained for such eventualities."*

Well, you wouldn't, would you.

BEAR IT IN MIND

The Gwent Criminal Justice Board offered the citizens of Abergavenny some sound seasonal advice: *"Remember that if someone is trying to pick a fight, they may not be thinking rationally due to the effect of too much alcohol."*

SHUTTING THE STABLE DOOR

Chris Rundle of the Western Daily Press surmised on how modern regulations might impact on the arrival of Mary and Joseph at their Bethlehem inn:

"Within hours of them moving in, someone would grass on the landlord and he'd get a visit from a jobsworth accusing him of converting an agricultural building into living accommodation without planning consent. A housing officer would declare the habitation unfit and issue a closing order, and a fire service inspection would insist on the straw being moved outside and the exit being clearly marked and fitted with appropriate emergency lighting. A health visitor would express horror at a child being kept in such insanitary conditions and recommend that the baby be taken into care and its parents prosecuted."

LOUSY MESSAGE

Over done it on the drinking and eating fronts?

How can you be sure if that's what's making you feel awful? You might have early symptoms of potentially fatal meningitis or septicemia, pointed out the Meningitis Research Foundation in their seasonal advice.

See – you're starting to get things in perspective already.

BAD PRESS

Butlins at Bognor Regis refused to accommodate TV's 'Flog It' host Paul Martin, when he was in town recording the collectibles programme. Paul had wanted to do a feature item on holiday camp memorabilia: Billy Butlin badges and the like.

The Butlins PR people declared that this wasn't the sort of publicity they wanted. Trips down memory lane to the old Red Coat days conveyed the wrong impression about the modern resort facility.

We can therefore only imagine how those spin wonks must have felt about the half page photograph of the entrance to the camp below the headline 'Xmas Evil' in a Boxing Day tabloid. The article was a round up of Christmas Day murders, and more than halfway through the gruesome summary of sundry stabbings across the country, readers eventually got to the case of a man dying from a heart attack following a family brawl at the camp.

After that hellish exposure, you can bet the Butlins team were wishing they hadn't let slip ten heavenly BBC minutes of Paul oozing over old knobbly knee contests.

HOME ALONE

Barbara Ellen argued persuasively in last year's Boxing Day Observer for the pleasures of spending Christmas Day alone – if only others would let you get on with it and not feel obliged to beg you to join them in their cheesy festive activities:

"It's as if you've gone from being a proper grown-up to a crippled Victorian orphan gnawing coal in an unheated scullery."

You know, a good book (no, not this one), whilst making yourself sick with a box of crystallised fruit, doesn't sound so bad when you think about it.

"Let's see. I've got a hundred and fifty three, and you've got one, in what looks suspiciously like your handwriting!"

HEADLINES AND DEADLINES

As one would expect, the newspapers prior to Christmas are rich in feature articles offering good advice on shopping, cooking, office etiquette and family behaviour. Doubtless editors dig deep to discover fresh material that will constitute a witty seasonal page, plus opportunities to illustrate same with glittery girls in party frocks.

Mostly they succeed exceedingly well, but occasionally there are disconcerting flaws in the flow and the end result just doesn't quite add up.

WATCH THOSE WHALES

The University of Wales estimated that Britons on average gain 5 pounds in weight over Christmas. So, if you were to add all that fat together nationally, it would amount to 15 million stone.

To make that concept more digestible to its readers, one regional paper (not situated near a coastline) explained that this would be equivalent to having 68 blue whales appear in their catchment area.

You can imagine that, can't you?

NEWSHOUNDS

One small Midlands city weekly devoted a December page to investigative journalism that revealed: "*Pets add to the enjoyment of Christmas for the older and younger members of the family, with over a fifth of pet owners saying their pet is a great source of stress relief.*"

Well, that must have made readers sit up and think.

And the in-depth reporting didn't end there: "*Three-quarters of the UK's cats and dogs will be eagerly waiting by the Christmas tree for their very own Christmas cards and gifts this year.*"

How many pets did the newshounds sniff out?

The fearless field team also tracked down the fact that one in five animal owners spend up to £50 on their special pets.

Examining the picture nationally, it emerged that cats and dogs in the South East are not so lucky as those in Scotland, because four out of every five Home County furries may not be receiving a treat this year.

How come a local paper can commit so many journalistic resources to a single article?

Oh, hang on, there's a line in there that reveals it was all culled from a Pedigree Pet Foods press release.

GIVE UNCLE A FLASH

One tabloid team of medical experts offered readers a handy hamper of lifestyle advice on how to survive the stress of Christmas Day, including: "*Why not try wearing reindeer antlers or flashing earrings*" to stimulate conversation with your elderly relatives.

ROCKY HORROR

A respected rock journalist joined in the seasonal shenanigans by penning an article claiming that having Number One hits at Christmas proved a curse for the bands concerned.

The piece identified the alarming fact that three deaths followed a brief December spell at Number One:

Run DMC ran up a winner with 'Christmas in Hollis' in 1987 and just 13 years later Jam Master Jay was shot dead.

Nun Jeanine Decker delivered a stunner as the Singing Nun with 'Dominique' in 1963 and merely 22 years later she committed suicide.

Are you starting to see the pattern?

Finally, confirming the revered rock and roll reviewer's thesis that bad things happen in threes, Bing Crosby first performed 'White Christmas' in 1942 and almost immediately... well, 33 years later... he died.

Em, that was of old age.

We don't think the fatal curse concept really holds up.

STAMP DOWN

One regional evening newspaper decided to put Royal Mail to the test by posting letters at 5.30pm one afternoon, then analysing their arrival times at various destinations dependent on the use of either first or second class stamps.

Results were somewhat inconclusive.

At most letterboxes both the first and second class letter arrived two days later; the rest were either one day better or worse.

A spokesman for Royal Mail pointed out the sample was a little on the small size.

In all, just 30 letters.

STIFF ONE

I saw in one paper that a gardener was using liquid Viagra to keep his Christmas tree fresh. That's just bollocks, isn't it?

Steve Manders, London

WHAT ARE THEY FOR?

One tabloid helpfully offered tips to women wondering how to pull men at Christmas parties: *"Men can't help ogling boobs. It is thought that this is because breasts are a sexual signal to help compensate for the buttocks not being so prominently displayed."*

THE PRICE OF A POLE DANCER

On the twelfth day of Christmas, my true love bought for me... here's a good vein for contemporary assessments of cost and inconvenience if we literally pursue the logic of the ditty.

The Daily Mail's Money Mail team tackled the issue with wisdom and good taste. Liz Phillips quoted figures from the Agricultural Wages Board to indicate the economics of managing milk maids, then sketched out a business plan (itemising changing rooms, rehearsal space, a rehearsal director, choreography, travel, food, bottled water and royalties for the music) for hiring the Rambert Dance Company to provide aesthetically pleasing Nine Ladies Dancing.

Whereas at the bottom end of the tabloid spectrum, readers could learn about eight milkmaid lingerie outfits (appropriately illustrated); and nine writhing pole dancers (also appropriately illustrated).

MANY USEFUL VIEWS

The Bad Christmas winning entry for getting most name checks in articles about business matters goes to senior financial adviser Martin Haigh.

He managed to get himself mentioned in six separate articles in the business pages of a regional newspaper.

And guess how many editions of the paper emerged before he reached that winning figure?

One.

Yes, a double-page spread on Christmas financial issues made half-a-dozen name-check references to the man himself, every time explaining what his job was, and what firm he worked for.

We tried to tell him in person about his winning exposure, but he didn't want to speak to us.

Maybe he's gone a bit shy after all that publicity.

We're sending him a copy of this for Christmas.

THEY DIDN'T WANT TO DO IT

All power to the Sun for promoting traditional Christian values at Christmas.

To make the point they mounted a Nativity scene on the back of a lorry and drove it round London.

The principle was good, but the practice seemed weak.

I don't know where they had recruited their actors from, but there was a certain lack of conviction in their eyes.

Some were dressed up as Wise men, but they looked more like depressed men to me. The most cheerful face was that of a big stuffed donkey.

Martin Fiennes, Slough

TIME RUNNING OUT

Our prize for making an early start on Christmas goes to the Whitsuntide edition of the Christian Malford Parish News (Christian Malford's a place, not a religion). There, in June, we discovered a request for knitters to get stuck into scarves, hats and mittens for Operation Christmas Child shoe box gifts. *"The accessories can be any shape, colour and design."* Contact the Editor for the *"teddies for tragedies"* pattern. What sort of pattern would that be? Let's not go there.

PAPARAZZI PRESSURE

Pity the screen stars who just want to nip down to the local shop for a pint of milk on a day off over Christmas.

There's always the danger of an unscrupulous freelance photographer stalking your home, hoping for a candid shot.

And it's not rocket science – just a matter of timing.

Sooner or later the celeb will emerge from their front door – and you just have to get that uncontrived look on the end of your lens for them to come across as gloomy losers, once it's blown up with a bit of copy about their good old days alongside.

Singer Tom Jones was on the receiving end of the "doesn't he look awful!" routine for having been snapped carrying a plastic carrier bag in Los Angeles. How unstagelike can the man be?

Leslie Grantham got the treatment with a vengeance, the broken spirit of Dirty Den seemingly sullenly stepping out of his lonely apartment. We invited him to explain how it feels, but he was too sick, sore or sour to respond.

PAPER THIN

Shopping is good for you, explained the Derby Express the day before Christmas Eve. *"Carrying two bags weighing 10 kilos while walking briskly for half an hour can burn 200 calories."*

NEW MEDIA, NEW FACTS

If you get fed up with the nonsense in the daily newspapers, you can always get some electronic advice from the internet.

A visit to one website exposed us to these handy tips:

Ladders feature greatly in home improvement accidents. For putting tinsel around your picture frames, a small collapsible ladder will do.

A smoke alarm is the easiest way to alert you to the turkey burning. Make sure it carries the kite mark (the alarm, not the turkey).

80% of people own smoke alarms, however not all actually function, which makes them pointless.

SURREAL SANTA PHOTO AWARD

Our prize for the strangest image of Santa to grace the pages of a newspaper article goes to the Gloucestershire Forester. Next to columnist George Fletcher's description of Finland's propensity for blood sports there's a photograph of a bespectacled Santa swimming across a lake with a wicker basket on his back.

Great article and a great picture, but we couldn't quite see how they went together.

So we're sending George and the Editor a free copy of this book.

"I don't know why you waste your time doing those stupid competitions in the paper!"

KISS GOODBYE TO THE MISTLETOE

Patently our contemporary commercial Christmas is a highly unenvironmental activity.

If you were to opt out of all seasonal undertakings you could give yourself a pat on the back for what you have done on behalf of future generations. Because the fact is we are eating up the earth's resources at far too fast a rate, and the environment would benefit greatly from a freeze regards Christmas. (Who said: This book's not helping?)

Of course, a huge proportion of our economic activity is driven by the Christmas season.

Factories and shops depend on it.

Farms devoted to turkeys and trees rely completely on this annual market.

But could we go for a simpler Christmas that didn't demand the consumption of massive resources?

WHAT A WASTE

The Christmas Resistance Movement recommends the end of compulsory consumption. "*We show our love for friends and family by giving our time and care, not by purchasing consumer goods.*"

Christmas creates an additional 3 million tonnes of waste over and above our normal weekly rubbish mountain.

A GIFT FOR FUTURE GENERATIONS

2 million Brits will help bring about irreversible changes to the environment over Christmas by flying abroad in search of sun or snow.

The airlines always look forward to massive business thanks to those with plenty of disposable income.

Every aircraft flight damages the planet by alarming amounts. A full jumbo jet round trip from London to Miami churns out 2,415 kg of carbon dioxide for every passenger aboard.

Those thoughtless fun-lovers hanging around Heathrow, Luton and Gatwick bleating about delayed departures are on the brink of delivering enormously destructive amounts of greenhouse gas into the earth's upper atmosphere.

Happy holiday.

GET ETHICAL

Leo Hickman and Jane Crinnion pursued an ethical audit documented in the Guardian in December 2004 by addressing the environmental horrors of the season: 200,000 trees are felled to create Britain's 1,700,000,000 Christmas cards and a further 40,000 get chopped down to produce 8,000 tonnes of wrapping paper.

And this is all before we've bought a gift.

Leo and Jane attempted to only do things that wouldn't leave a negative environmental footprint.

Compelling accounts of their endeavours in the excellent Eden books 'A life stripped bare' and 'A good life'.

They fearlessly and candidly tackled the big issues, and some little ones too, such as: You should avoid advent calendars with a chocolate behind each door.

See, you hadn't thought about that, had you!

BOTTLE BRUSH SCRUBS UP AGAIN

How green is felling millions of precious trees each year to stick in your living room for a fortnight before dumping them at the tip?

Stinks, doesn't it, when you think about it.

So we salute Doreen Hardcastle who uses the same Christmas tree she's had since childhood.

Her 1930s wooden-pole tree with metal arms is still going strong.

In fact her decoration is well on its way to being an antique.

Not sure it would scrub up well enough for e-bay however.

The scoffers describe it as resembling a giant bottle brush.

She sees what they mean, but she doesn't care.

Good on you, Marian. If there were more people like you around, the planet wouldn't be in the mess it's in.

CARD MOUNTAIN

I read that the Woodland Trust organises Christmas card recycling. Bins are provided in branches of Tesco and WHSmiths during January, and last year 45 million were collected.

But that's less than three cards per household. What happened to all the rest? Do they go to landfill? I think it's better to recycle your cards by re-using them. Put a sticky white label over the writing inside and send it on to someone else next year.

William Ferndale, Newcastle-on-Tyne

12 DAYS OF CLIMATE CHANGE

Fifty years ago almost all the elements of our turkey dinner came from within a few square miles of our front door (in some instances reaching the High Street or market stall by horse and cart). Now your typical turkey dinner has run up 30,000 miles before reaching your table. The bird's buzzed in from Thailand, vegetables from Africa, wine from down-under, point out the Soil Association. Only the Brussels sprouts won't have come from far afield.

So as we toast tradition and celebrate our good fortune, let's try to forget that our meal has given the poor old planet a right kicking. The food chain causes a fifth of the UK's emissions of carbon dioxide, and each calorie of overseas fresh fruit and vegetable on your plate used up 66 calories of fuel to air freight it to you. Cheers.

MISTLETOE NO MORE

Every year without fail the camera crews would turn up and turn over. It was the day of the annual mistletoe auction in tiny Tenbury Wells on the very west of Worcestershire. It was a tradition as old as television itself.

Mm, possibly older.

Alas, a major media tragedy has struck, and thus this reliable gig on the news crew calendar is no more.

Last year the auction house abandoned the event due to lack of available product and brutal, uncaring competition from overseas.

British mistletoe is on the decline. We have climate change to thank for that.

Consequently very few itinerant mistletoe collectors have been gathering the stuff up to take to Tenbury mid-December. Even the most predatory hedgerow scavenger could not find enough to make it worth his while.

Meanwhile foreign entrepreneurs had realised that synthetic mistletoe could be manufactured and shipped into Britain at a fraction of the cost of the real thing.

(Why didn't they get the migrant workers in Spain to grow mistletoe under plastic then send it on polystyrene trays to Britain, like the lettuce leaves rinsed in raw sewage? Don't know).

Anyway, back to Tenbury.

All this change is not just affecting the environment and shopping habits but individual lives and prospects.

Office worker Margaret had been employed at the auctioneers for nearly fifty years. The mistletoe event was the high point of her work calendar. Last year the firm made her redundant.

Think of poor old Margaret when you're snogging someone under a strand of cheap Chinese mock mistletoe.

"Eric, you're not having the same thing again.
You had sex last Christmas."

BAD SANTAS

Who'd be a Father Christmas? Far from a delightful fantasy function as homely heart warmer and generous present-giver, the role can be a potential disaster area. Here are some very good reasons to keep out of that big red suit.

SANTA VERSUS SLAYMAKER

Slaymaker – sounds like the name of a comic book villain, but in fact he's a Welsh policeman.

One Sunday evening last December, PC Gareth Slaymaker was out in force – with baton drawn and CS gas at the ready - to deal with a gang of drunken Santas.

Yes, a terrible notion, but it's true.

The aggressive Father Christmases were in a pub in Newtown in north Wales, having had too much to drink.

They were the ragged remnants of a huge body of runners from a fun race.

Over 4,000 Santas had turned up in the town to take part in the event.

And after all that exercise, some needed liquid refreshment.

Sadly, instead of taking the recommended sherry-with-mince-pie route for travelling Santas, a number of them picked the pint of bitter option, at the end of which another beer seemed the logical place to go, after which the third beckoned and so on.

Then, in the best traditions of British binge drinking, they started to fall out with each other. Over what we may never know.

Sleigh servicing? Chimney footholds? Reindeer feed prices? Nasty nippers hogging grottos and demanding bigger presents?

Whatever – poor Newtown faced the ugly sight of brawling Father Christmases. Not something children should be exposed to.

So Community Safety Officer Gary Slaymaker was summoned to give the offending Santas an ear-bending.

This was not the spirit of Christmas.

Oh, no, no, no.

RUBBISH

There's a dustbin man in Worcester who dresses up as Santa in the weeks prior to Christmas.

What are kids supposed to make of that? Is this the man from the grotto who will be coming down the central heating vent on Christmas Eve, looking forward to his mince pie before dumping the contents of his plastic refuse sack on to the carpet?

Surely youngsters would be horrified if this fellow entered the house and caused Mum to have to spend Christmas hoovering?

Peter Slater, Upton on Severn

SHOCKING SANTA

I was shocked to hear my children were subjected to lessons from a green Santa in their junior school classroom.

Yes, white beard and black boots, but green suit instead of the red.

When they first told me about it, I assumed it was some environmentally aware Father Christmas warning about the global repercussions of our consumerism through the season of excess.

But no, he was a public relations agent for a big electricity supply firm, tasked with winning tiny hearts and minds to believe in the virtues of power supply from the firm when they grow up.

In my opinion, tradition was being abused for commerce, with the tacit approval of head teachers.

Mavis Summerton, Hereford

BREAK DOWN

A widower took on the role of Santa in a shopping arcade in Wigan. He was short on training and not in the best of spirits. A toddler slipped off the man's knee and banged its head on the floor. The child began to howl, and soon the Santa was crying too, full of shame at his clumsiness, and pain over his loneliness. The baby was given an x-ray and declared to be fine. Solutions to the state of the Santa may take longer.

YOUR PRESENT WILL BE IN THE POST

My brother Jack was driving through a town in southern California and was mystified by the sight of a Santa Claus at the side of the road. He slowed down to see what was going on and discovered it was a police officer doing speed checks.

Gayle Mantob, San Francisco

PICTURE THIS

You've got a run down, money-losing restaurant in the back end of Lapland with not enough through-put of custom.

What do you do? Turn it into a McDonalds franchise?

Yes, you're close to despair. But then someone suggests a marvellous money-making scheme.

Lapland. Just think about it. This is where Father Christmas lives, isn't it.

Oh, yes.

Why not set up a service for rich kids from England to come over and meet Santa on his home patch?

They'd never go for it. They can see Santa down the road at their local department store for nothing.

Think big. People with too much disposable income don't know what to do with it next. A bit of branding and marketing and they'll beat a path to your rustic wooden door.

And so, within a month, it was all set up.

And, yes, the principle worked. People in Britain were prepared to pay hundreds of pounds to fly to Lapland and stick their kids on Santa's knee for a few seconds.

Brilliant.

But then one day Santa took a turn for the worse. He wasn't well, maybe hung-over, cheesed off – who knows. But he wouldn't do the business.

Locked up the grotto and cleared off with the key.

And blow me, there's a coach load of kids with their bleating parents hanging around, straight off the package flight, demanding their brats get a face-to-face photographable moment with the man himself.

You make excuses. He's too busy.

Come back next year.

But these bolshie British Mums and Dads are not easily fobbed off. They have invested nearly £500 per head to get their moment with the real Lapland

Santa.

So another member of staff is forced into the big red suit. And in a corner of the kitchen at the back of the restaurant, he takes his place on the chair, ready for the photographs. (There won't be any cuddly chit-chat about what we are hoping for on Christmas Day, because this fellow speaks no English.)

Eventually the tired and tiresome youngsters are briefly ushered in and sit on the reluctant fellow's knees, and have their snap taken.

But what's that in the back of the shot? Only dirty dishes in the sink, plus a plastic ketchup bottle.

So when the families return home they kick up a stink, and get the newspapers to publish the pictures of their kids surrounded by grimy utensils and slimy sauce bottles with a sheepish, silent Santa stuck in the middle.

"We thought he looked shifty as soon as we walked in there," one aggrieved adult told us.

Perhaps those enterprising Laplanders will now take another careful look at that McDonalds option.

THE PIG, THE TRUMPET AND SANTA

Across the road from us is a popular drinking hole, The Pig and Trumpet.

It's not too noisy and people normally disperse without any trouble, but on Christmas Eve they had a special guest up on the roof, who needed the fire brigade to get him down.

Santa had had a few pints and had climbed out of a window and got up on the roof. I wish my niece, Nancy, had been here. She would have loved it.

We couldn't believe it when we looked out the window to see the fire brigade hoisting a ladder up to the roof so that one of their men could help the Santa down. He was definitely drunk and disorderly, and in no fit state to deliver presents.

Mrs Bellow, Wednesbury

FIZZING AND COUGHING

St. Nicholas was not over-weight.

Victorian Santas seemed to have had no trouble climbing down chimneys swept by youngsters. So when did the man get fat?

American advertising agencies came up with an image of Mister Claus to market "soda" in the 1930s. The picture they chose was of a jolly, bulging-cheeked fellow - before the concept of obese had caught on.

Then another American illustrator had the eye-watering idea of giving Santa a tobacco pipe.

Yes, a smoking Father Christmas was a familiar sight for many years in the pages of American magazines.

Might seem barmy now, but remember cuddly Bing Crosby was frequently sucking on a smelly briar between his songs and kisses in the film 'White Christmas'.

The nicotine-addicted version of Santa died off some years ago.

We wonder why.

WHEN SANTA WENT ALL WONKY

We took our kids to the Christmas Fair at their Junior School. It was a lovely atmosphere until Father Christmas appeared, and abruptly collapsed on the floor.

Teachers and parents rushed to the rescue.

He was carried into the staff room, and an ambulance was called.
Meanwhile lots of Mums and Dads were trying to answer awkward questions from their offspring, mostly along the lines of: "Will he be better in time for Christmas at our house?"

Jim and Marion Jones, Basingstoke

FILM FLOP

You've got a video rental shop, and coming up to Christmas you put all the seasonal titles on a special shelf near the front as ideal options for a family treat one evening. (Okay, maybe not a treat, but a joint activity to bond everyone together for an hour and a half. Oh, all right then, just something to keep the kids quiet for a while so the adults can get on with… whatever.)

Anyway, of all the movies made for the season, which one was hired out the least?

'Santa Claus conquers the Martians'. This 1964 flick tells of Father Christmas making a long and hazardous journey to the Red Planet, where, after a series of heart-stopping set-backs, he brings delight and gifts to Martian offspring (presumably they would be especially small little green men).

Psychologists might do well to see if there is evidence that George Bush Junior was exposed to this mind-bending epic during his formative years.

SACKED SANTA

A one man show, with no curtain, no script, and a serious shortage of props. That was what actor Philip Mead faced, when he commenced what proved to be a rather short season starring at a department store in Norwich.

The mature entertainer had signed up for the role of Santa back in the summer. He was promised a golden throne, and support from a couple of elves.

He invested £400 in an up-market Santa suit, seeing this as the start of a new career, after working in clubs and holiday camps for many years.

But when the big day arrived, there was no sign of the throne, nor the elves for that matter.

He was on his own, and was expected to wander round the toy department, dishing out small novelties to little children.

"Where the 'ell are the elves?" 16-stone Philip demanded to know.

Alas, the plan had changed, and no-one had told the regional secretary of the actors' union, Equity – who was soon examining his terms and conditions.

Fact was he towered over the tots, and some seemed alarmed at the great big bloke in the bright red suit.

A throne would bring him down to eye height. Suitably supervised, he could then take a couple of youngsters on his knee. And hear them whisper in his ear what they expected to see in their stockings on Christmas Day.

Wouldn't you have thought the furniture department could have rustled up an end-of-range sofa done up in silver foil – okay, not a throne of gold, but along the right lines.

But no, the store bosses had other ideas. They just wanted their Lapland rep to hang round the tills, filling the gaps between the kids nagging their parents into shelling out a fortune for some terrible electronic game advertised on TV. Well, for someone with trade unionism in his heart, this was not on.

Philip demanded to speak to those in authority, and the managing director no less soon scuttled from his office to attend to this potentially ugly scene in front of the unsold chess sets.

Philip was asked to leave. Fuming, he did. Then locals kicked up a stink.

They picketed the premises. Philip offered to return to his role, but the shop had now picked up a cheap substitute from the dole queue.

Some good news though: "Peachy" Mead's career got a massive boost from this event. For the first time in his life he'd achieved big write-ups in the papers, he's been signed up as Christmas entertainer at a Norfolk hotel, and he's doing a roaring trade in after-dinner speeches about becoming Britain's Number One Sacked Santa.

NO HARM IN A QUICK ONE

I was once a very bad Santa.

I agreed to being the Father Christmas for our small department store's seasonal festivities.

For fifteen consecutive days (excluding Sundays) I would sit in the grotto and talk to kids about their Christmas wishes.

Well, I love children, which is good, but I also smoke, which is bad.

I told the manager of the store about my need to pop out for a cigarette every hour or so, which he said wouldn't be a problem. It was just a matter of another member of staff minding the grotto during my brief absences off to "smoker's corner" in the car park behind the premises.

Things went well for the first few days, and there was always someone around to stop kids helping themselves to the goodies in my grotto whilst I enjoyed a fag round the back. But the demands on other staff grew as Christmas drew closer, and so I was having to wait longer for my break, or beg someone to keep an eye on the grotto so I could satisfy my cravings. I didn't get the impression anyone resented me nipping out, it was just they were all pretty busy themselves, which was good for the family firm.

One day I couldn't find anyone to cover for me, so, as there were no kids around, I lit a sly cigarette in the back of the grotto (ignoring the no smoking policy on the premises).

After a few minutes I was back on duty, with no harm done. I stupidly decided this was the way forward and so stopped asking shop assistants to man the fort. Instead I waited for a quiet patch and had a quick drag.

Then the inevitable happened. A mum turned up with her little ones, who expected some quality time with Santa. I swiftly stubbed out my cigarette and started to chat to the youngsters about what they hoped I'd deliver on Christmas Day.

The kids were enchanted, Mum was pleased, and then I saw the smoke rising from the crepe paper around my grotto. The cigarette obviously hadn't gone out and had instead started to smoulder. I pushed the children away and tried to smother the flames, but it was amazing how swiftly they rose. Mercifully another member of staff responded to the commotion very quickly and grabbed a fire extinguisher and sprayed foam on the fire.

The grotto was saved, along with the whole of the store. But I had let down the brotherhood of Father Christmases very badly.

Bob Galloway, Belfast

THE STUPID CLUB

This club exists all through the year, but at Christmas it takes on a special seasonal quality and is temporarily joined by people who at other times of the year might be refused membership for being too sensible.

Amongst recent honorary members are:

Adam Darby of Burntwood in Staffordshire. For doing a water ski jump in the nude on Boxing Day. Flying off a ramp at 35 mph into the freezing cold of Chasewater reservoir.

And a warm welcome, please, to the committee of the Cannock Women's Institute, whose Christmas party consisted of a demonstration of synchronised swimming – in a function room. The ladies donned swimming costumes and hair caps before standing in a row behind a blue cloth, waving artificial legs in the air to indicate what might be happening under water.

WHAT'S THAT NUMBER AGAIN?

Hereford & Worcester Ambulance Service face three problems over the holiday period: alcohol, alcohol and alcohol. "*Over-indulging is effectively an over-dose,*" explained control room manager Mike Clarke. Alcohol is also a key factor in domestic disputes and assaults. Nearly 40% of Mike's staff have been on the receiving end of harassment or abuse from drunk patients, and almost 20% have suffered abuse from the drunken relatives of patients. And if all that wasn't enough, the service gets calls from drunks who can't afford a taxi home and think an ambulance would be just the job.

Apart from alcohol, the other big trigger for emergency medical attention is indigestion - which the indulgent sufferer imagines may be a heart attack or the onset of cancer. Well, you do, don't you.

But most annoying are people with toothache who don't bother going to the dentist before Christmas because they're too busy shopping or partying.

We're not dentists, pointed out the long-suffering A&E staff. "*We give them some painkillers and send them on their way to leave space for the true emergencies – the ones spilling blood in the foyer.*"

DRINK UP

At our Christmas office party a lad of eighteen who had just joined the firm walked into the bar and saw the boss's brandy on the counter. For some inexplicable reason, this lad said: "Oh look, one of those joke shop glasses." He picked it up and made a vigorous gesture of throwing the contents at our boss. Patently the brandy went all over the boss's tie, shirt and suit, and the lad stood there amazed that it wasn't a joke shop glass from which the liquid couldn't escape, but a genuine glass of brandy.

He left the firm - for some allegedly unconnected reason - by mid January.

Mark Havant, Taunton

ALL LIT UP

Two Manchester professional footballers fell out during their Christmas party. One tried to set fire to the other's T-shirt – whilst he was wearing it. But this prank backfired when the other player's cigar accidentally poked the first man in the eye.

One all, then.

NOT PART OF THE PLAN

You run a Range Rover, which is proving horribly heavy on fuel. Imagine your delight when someone tells you there's a big tank full of diesel which is "surplus to requirements". It's at a Powys health centre, and apparently they'll have to discard the fuel unless someone can take it away.

So naturally you help yourself. But someone spots you at it. And it turns out the fuel wasn't up for grabs, and the police reckon you've committed a crime.

You're deeply aggrieved by this misunderstanding and challenge the court proceedings. You don't turn up for the hearing, as you don't accept the charges. But these frustrating factors are lost on Llandrindod magistrates who hear the case on December 22nd, and send you down for 14 days.

Christmas and New Year behind bars. And you're not even allowed to keep the fuel!

PARTY PANTS

Our office party took place at a nightclub, and we all had a right good rave-up. The place is on the bank of a canal. I had been there before, but when I came out of the venue at about two that morning, distinctly worse for wear, I was absolutely convinced that the surface of the canal was a walkway. So I started to take a shortcut to the taxi rank and in seconds was under water wondering what had happened.

The bouncers dragged me out, and my mates then helped me out of my wet clothes. One of them threw my underpants up in the air and they landed on a roof. Next day at work I got some serious ribbing, not least because my pants were still visible on the building next to the nightclub.

I was very tempted to get a ladder the next evening and rescue my embarrassing underwear.

Mercifully they had disappeared by the start of the New Year.

Where did they go? We'll never know.

Sam Willoughby, Reading

PINT DUTY

You're a police officer responsible for traffic in South Wales. Coming up to Christmas, you've made a substantial contribution to the anti-drink drive campaign.

Time to relax, and have a quick one. Then back in the car, but blow me if that's not a breathalysing team up ahead.

Your colleagues stop you, and – yep, you're over the limit. So much for promotion next year.

CRUISING

Christmas Day early afternoon and it's time for you to drive along Interstate 44 to head for your sister's home with presents for her and the kids.

Good road, great car – with cruise control.

Yes, why bother with that tiresome accelerator pedal (sorry, gas pedal) when you've got one of these hi-tech bits of trickery in your motoring arsenal?

Just set it at 55 mph, sit back and turn up the Christmas music on the radio, and sail along.

Mm, nice and easy.

So smooth, you could fall asleep – which is exactly what the lady did.

However she woke up with one heck of a jolt on hitting a parked vehicle at the side of the road. She was jammed inside and the car was filling with smoke. Mercifully someone stopped and managed to pull her out of the broken window seconds before the vehicle caught on fire, and she got out of the accident with just bruises.

Stuff cruise control, poor woman spent Christmas dealing with bruise control.

TELL US ABOUT YOUR CUSTOMS

How can you smuggle cigarettes into Britain? Well, it's all a matter of picking the right place and the right time.

Forget about Heathrow or Dover.

You've got to get off the beaten track a bit – like Newcastle Airport up in out-of-the-way Northumberland.

And when can you be sure of a quiet day there? Why Christmas Day, of course. Excellent plan.

So it's just a matter of stuffing a suitcase or two full of fags, and slipping them past the dozy staff.

Well, the gang might have got away with that, but they made one tiny error.

Instead of a couple of cases they tried to sneak 146 items of tobacco-packed luggage off the carousel.

And – surprise, surprise – someone noticed.

THE GRAVITATIONAL DISEASE

An American medical research agency undertook an in-depth study.

What health problem might they have seen fit to address?

No, not AIDS, or polio, or even the common cold.

Instead they applied their energy to Christmas Decorating Dangers.

"*Be careful you don't fall off a ladder*", was their conclusion after an intense study of – yes, you've got it - accidents up ladders.

Almost 2 million Yanks have a fall each year, and around one per cent of these are Christmas decorating-related.

The boffins at the lab cleverly allocated the months of November, December and January to define the boundaries for their body of evidence about people who had been up a ladder and had come down in a hurry, but not by the rungs.

And what did they come up with?

"*Hanging lights, and mounting and decorating trees are two common activities that lead to falls,*" they concluded.

Who said American scientists aren't making valuable contributions to international understanding?

GOING DOWN

My girlfriend had gone down to the south coast to see her folks for Christmas, and when she came back the day after Boxing Day, I decided to take her for a drink to a smart hotel. She turned up looking absolutely gorgeous and sexy. We had a couple of drinks and I was desperate to make love to her. We couldn't go back to my place as my flatmate had some of his family round for the day. I was thinking about investing in a room in the hotel for a couple of hours but £160 seemed steep. We got in the lift and took a ride up to the top floor. We started kissing in the lift, and I could feel her stockings and suspenders through her dress, which really turned me on. We got to the top floor and walked along the corridor in the vain hope that there might be an empty bedroom open where we could nip in for ten minutes. But no luck.

We got back in the lift and I pressed the close door button, and then kept it pressed while also pressing the top floor button, which seemed to keep the lift on the top floor with the door closed. This was about the best privacy we could hope for, and whilst it wasn't easy making love with one hand on the two lift buttons, I pressed on, so to speak.

We were in the midst of our love-making when the lift door suddenly slid open. I was at the point of no return, but a security guy yanked me out, causing me to make a mess on the carpet.

We dressed on the landing and were escorted down the stairs and told to never come back.

Ted, Boston

SEARCHING THE BOTTOM

What were people trying to find out about on their internet search engines during the last twelve months?

An in-depth analysis by subject revealed that the sixth most searched topic was football, fifth was the BBC's 'East Enders', in fourth position was horoscopes, and taxing us all by surprise at Number Three: the Inland Revenue.

Pipped at the post for top position was Channel Four's 'Big Brother'. And what did the pipping? Pornography.

WHERE'S THAT COME FROM?

What I want for the New Year is liposuction, said a quarter of women surveyed about their weight after Christmas. Ten per cent were prepared to have their stomachs stapled.

What did they blame the problem on? Alcohol, takeaways and chocolate.

WHAT A WAY TO GO

Has a Santa ever got stuck in a chimney?

We hope not, because it isn't a pleasant experience.

The American Journal of Forensic Science reported the case of a burglar who became trapped in a chimney and died due to postural asphyxia associated with inhalational and burn injuries.

(More results of improbable research at: www.improbable.com)

THAT SHEILA'S NO SHEILA

You're a transvestite, always on the look out for some nice women's clothes. But it's so embarrassing wandering into boutiques with your deep voice, 5 o'clock shadow and lumpy things in your underpants.

Then you hit on the idea of retrieving female attire from those charity bins which recycle clothes.

Excellent concept.

Stick your arm through the flap and pull out something feminine.

This is what one devious fellow was up to on Christmas Day in Sydney. He tried on a mini-skirt and felt it looked promising.

Wanting a blouse to go with it, he pushed his head into the bin and got it jammed.

Police officers had to rescue him. So much for keeping a low profile.

STEPPING OUT GINGERLY

I was told a good hangover cure was ginger. So I tipped the contents of a packet of ginger powder into a cup, poured in some warm water and drank it. This was a bad thing to do. I vomited for about four hours.

Never again.

Miles Stephens, London

WHAT ABOUT THE WORKERS?

Who works hardest at Christmas?

Well, if you believe in Santa, then he's got the most demanding task, travelling million of miles at the speed of light to deliver presents for every child on Christmas Eve.

Next to him come Mums, no question of it.

Graft and a half.

One Norwegian woman was so determined to get away from it all, she walked on her own to the South Pole in 1994.

Okay, Liv Arnesen went into the history books… but we reckon she just did it to avoid the tinsel application, gift decision-making, turkey preparation and festive TV programming….

DOING A FOREIGNER

Pity the poor Royal Mail staff – snowed under with letters and cards to deliver. They have too much on their plate.

That must be what the Inland Revenue were thinking when they decided to hand over one hundred thousand items of overseas mail to a Swedish postal service for delivery around the world, thus saving the UK taxpayer a few thousand pounds.

Oh yes, and possibly putting a British postman or two out of work.

GET YOUR CARDS

Having a job's a lot better than not having one, but the firm I worked for really took advantage of us at Christmas.

We were producing chip and pin cards and the roll-over to this technology was planned to happen at the start of 2005, so there was a massive demand for our systems to be in place by the New Year.

Fair enough – it was the cutting edge of technology and commerce.

Everyone was working shifts and Saturday mornings were part of the regular week, but because Christmas Day fell on a Saturday, the firm wanted us to work over the previous weekend to make up hours but without any additional pay.

The only way we could have Christmas morning off work was by working the previous Saturday afternoon at normal rate.

So anyone who used their chip and pin card for the first time in the January sales, I hope they'll give us a thought as they press their numbers on to the keypad.

Irene Makepeace, Cheltenham

TOUGH IN TOYLAND

Spare a thought for those little workers helping Santa prepare his load.

Yes, Chinese employees in massive custom-built toy factories.

They are mostly women, and they mostly live in dormitories in compounds adjacent to the factories.

Many put in 70 hours a week to take away less than £10.

TALKING TURKEY

Five days prior to Christmas, one regional newspaper gently and diplomatically explained to readers that "a turkey's life cycle often ends this week."

What a life cycle, Mum?

It's that part of your existence before you're... slaughtered.
What's slaughtered?
How shall I put it? The meat for your dinner used to have feet and a head.
What happened to them, Mum?
They got cut off.
Why?
So it could fit in the oven.
Ah, a rational explanation at last.
Apparently, while we're happy to eat our way through 33 million turkeys each year, finding people willing to work in slaughter houses is very hard indeed.

GOOD WORK IF YOU CAN GET IT

There's a theory that obese people suffer from low self-esteem. Such folk have our sympathy – unless you're weighing in way over 20 stone but have a theatrical agent who fixes you up with Santa gigs across southern California come December.

Apparently there are a few hot properties in the 'playing Santa' stakes who can pull in thousands of dollars for the "Ho, Ho, Ho" routine, and are enjoying good "word-of-mouth" amongst the film star community.

Well, you know what celebs are like. They don't want just any gardener, they must have the guy who did Al Pacino's patio, or Cameron Diaz's dahlias.

So when it comes to Santas, they insist on the one who teased Vin Diesel, goosed Gwyneth Paltrow.

Feel for those fellas behind the cotton wool beard because the rest of the year their phone doesn't ring much. They seldom audition for drama series, they never become short-listed for Oscars. They're just not box office.

Do they care? Every year they do a lot of resting, then it's on with that red suit and white beard and down to the studio parties, to get a couple of sweet little starlets on their big fat knees.

So get off that sofa, fellas. Scrub yourself down, buy a red suit, and find an entertainment agent – preferably on Sunset Boulevard.

IT'S AN EDUCATION

Anyone contemplating pursuing a career in the field of Christmas stuff ought to consider a term or two at Santa School.

No, it's not a classroom with a blackboard and outside toilets somewhere near the North Pole.

It's a website, with segments devoted to Rules, a Training Manual and Q&A.

Our first Q would be: "Isn't Christmas about giving?" because the web pages are carefully labelled: 'All Rights Reserved'. "No part of this page may be reproduced without the permission of the copyright holder," which, of course, applies to this sentence, so we may have crossed the line of permissible behaviour.

The Safety Messages run to 12 pages, and cover lots of obvious things and a number of very obscure concepts, such as ground fault circuit interrupters, de-icing fuel lines with methyl hydrate, recalibrating your thermometer, and what to do if you accidentally set fire to yourself.

WHO NEEDS MEDICS

The Welsh St Johns Ambulance service - obviously keen to avoid unnecessary call outs during the holidays - offered those in trouble some tips on how to self-medicate:

"Choking on the turkey wishbone: if the casualty is breathing – then encourage them to cough." (Presumably if they're not breathing, then there's no point in encouraging them to do anything, and you might as well get on with the pudding.)

"Champagne cork explodes into someone's eye: Support the casualty's head on your knees. Tell them to keep their good eye still." (Em, as opposed to what? Waving it about?)

"Hypothermia whilst out: Put a hat on."

"Passing out and collapsing at a party: Kneel down and put their feet on your shoulders." (Oh, yeah?)

"Suspected broken bones? Go to your A&E using your own transport."

See, they don't want their Christmas spoilt, if they can avoid it!

ON YOUR WICK

The executives at Channel Five don't just figure out what programmes they should deliver to the nation's living rooms.

The suits (if they wear them) also believe in building better human relations – well, at least amongst their employees.

The popular broadcasting leadership decided their underlings needed team-inspiration and so got the troops to undertake exercises that would promote bonding and communication (as opposed to a few beers in a bar whilst knocking the boss).

One team tried to construct a Nativity scene from office stationery and other handy consumables - like straw and candles – of which there are always plenty inside Channel headquarters.

Well, any TV exec should know that such items don't go together.

It's like putting on the Queen's Speech in the centre break of Celebrity Love Island. Guess what happened?

Some would-be broadcasting wonk lit the candles and so set fire to the straw, which set off the alarms and necessitated an evacuation of the offices.

We were assured this would not be repeated.

SICK

Staff from two Birmingham hospitals competed with each other to come up with the most spectacular displays of Christmas decorations on the premises.

The Bed Management team from the City Hospital took first prize with a First World War-themed tableaux utilising suppositories as bullets.

Who said: "For all the good those weird-looking pills were doing me, I might as well have stuck them up my arse."?

NUMBERS GAME

One out of every six employees aged between 16 and 30 in the West Midlands admitted to having a sexual fling with someone at work during the pre-Christmas party season, one year at least. Less than half said they'd used a condom.

MOTHER CHRISTMAS

Woolworths polled 4,000 parents and discovered that there's a giant gender gap in the seasonal tasks.

Surprise, surprise.

Mums spend twice as much time shopping for Christmas stuff as men.

20% of women spend 5 hours decorating the Christmas tree, compared with just 1% of males who commit this amount of time to the activity.

Further fascinating finding: Many Mums would like more help from other members of the family with the seasonal chores. Oh, really?

Then, right at the end, one you weren't expecting: more sons than daughters help with cleaning up afterwards.

See, boys aren't all bad.

ACCESS BAGGAGE

Baggage handlers for an American airline staged a lightening strike at Christmas, and so the management decided to get passengers to their destinations without their associated suitcases.

Not everyone was happy with this decision. Things like a change of clothes and presents for your hosts are useful when you arrive somewhere for the holidays.

The airline had mountains of luggage in the wrong places and paid huge sums of money to taxi firms to deliver suitcases to individual addresses between Boxing Day and the New Year.

In more than one instance a suitcase arrived at the required address after the person it belonged to had already headed back in the other direction, and so some people didn't see their belongings until several weeks after they had checked their baggage in for their holiday flight.

PLUMBING NEW DEPTHS

Our central heating packed in on Christmas Day. Because we had my mother with us, I didn't think we could do without heat until after Boxing Day, so I called a plumbing service advertised in the Yellow Pages and a man said he would come round. I should have asked the price, but as it was Christmas and as it was my mother's welfare at stake I decided to treat it like an extra present for her.

The plumber turned up and was very pleasant and fiddled with the boiler for half an hour, then told us the price would be £200.

I wanted to argue with him. In fact I wanted to hit him, but because of my mother I wrote out a cheque.

I harbour a wish to bump into him in our supermarket and to give him a piece of my mind in front of everyone.

Jill Holbourne, Cambridge

HELP

For many people Boxing Day is a time to recover, relax, rest.

But not for those call centre operatives standing by to take incoming queries from new owners of computer equipment bought at Dixons, Currys and PC World.

A fresh plea for help reached the talented crew every 21 seconds during the day.

And what proved to be the most effective advice was: *"Plug it in properly, make sure it's switched on and follow the instructions provided."*

NOT FEELING TOO GOOD

Monday 27th December 2004 was the busiest day ever for the NHS Direct telephone advice service.

More than 29,000 people phoned to moan about coughs, flu-like symptoms, vomiting and diarrhoea. (In that descending order; of course, some may have had more than one of those symptoms. And some poor bastards may have had the whole lot.)

One man rang to say he feared his turkey was contaminated, to which the highly trained, diplomatic call operative replied: *"Don't eat it, then."*

SPELL IT OUT

The British Council saw fit to explain the principles of a "thriving business in the UK" to Russians in its newsletter: *"Although there are different stories, some of the same characters and elements turn up in most of them. The hero and heroine are both traditionally played by women.*

A scene where one character hides behind someone else, causing shouts of 'it's behind you' is common and there is usually a scene where someone gets covered in something unpleasant."

Yes, a pantomime.

TRYING TO HELP

You're a West Yorkshire paramedic, on standby to deal with any eventuality.

The call comes through that someone's collapsed at a party.

You and your mate head for the scene, determined to do your best for the man in distress.

You arrive and run into the house. It's all about assessing the incident, making space, planning your moves.

But the other party-goers don't appreciate your efforts. They tell you to clear off. You explain your intentions.

They don't seem to care, and want you out of the house.

Several of them become aggressive, and so you retreat back to your ambulance.

You report back to base that you can't make progress.

The police arrive and enter the house.

They can't find any collapsed party on the floor.

He must have recovered.

Okay, job done.

On to the next incident where you hope you'll get a better reception.

FEELING COMFORTABLE?

I was a trainee copywriter in an advertising agency in Leeds when my first Christmas in employment came along.

I got through the party without making too much of a fool of myself, but when it came to New Year's Eve things started to get out of hand. One of the Account Directors took to plying me with drink.

So he didn't have to drink and drive, he'd booked himself a room in the Holiday Inn up the road from our agency.

He invited some of us to join him in his room and make the most of the mini-bar. When people left the offices I assumed they were on their way to the hotel. I'd been to the toilet and so left the building on my own.

I headed up to the Holiday Inn and asked for the Director's room number. I knocked on the door and he let me in.

I looked round for other colleagues but there weren't any.

He told me to help myself to the contents of the mini-bar whilst he had a shower.

I sat watching TV and after a few minutes he emerged from the bathroom wearing just a towelling dressing gown.

He sat down on the bed next to me and only now did it dawn on me that he was gay and was about to seduce me.

I leapt up and ran from the room, not bothering to take my coat which had my wallet in it.

So I had to walk home in the freezing cold, which made me ill for several days. Neither he nor I mentioned the incident to anyone in the agency, though both of us carried on working there for several years.

Roger Garbet, Hastings

"To be quite honest, we were expecting a more substantial Christmas bonus."

THE THOUGHT THAT COUNTS

"Ever since I was a little child I wanted a Lamborghini," explained Mum.
So Hubby got her one for Christmas.
Life for lottery winners.
Mum was learning to drive. Let's hope this wasn't in the new motor.
What about a car for your dog?
No, you can't train pooch to drive.
But some swanky pet shops offered a pink dog basket shaped to look like a VW Beetle.
Or at the bottom end of the market you can buy special Christmas toilet roll.
Here are some more memorable gifts...

PUTTING YOUR FOOT IN IT

Retired train driver Bill Wardle is 66 and lives in warden-aided accommodation in Nottingham. Since 2002 he has been wheelchair bound, having had both legs amputated because of disease.
And what did the staff give him as a Christmas present? A pair of socks.
Matron Reenie Margold explained to us that on Christmas Eve they had had an agency nurse come along to help out when they were short staffed.
The presents had been individually picked for each resident, but the agency nurse got the labels mixed up.
They mean well, those agency nurses, but it's just not the same, is it!

FROG OFF

I am the victim of other people's terrible Christmas gifts. Our office is full of idiots who have ghastly mobile phone rings that blast off at all times of day. If you haven't heard one, they sound like: "Wheerdingwilwildododingdingblonkkkzizzizzizz!" There should be a law against it.

Doris Jackson, Wimbledon

THE PERFECT COUPLE

What do British men want to find in their Christmas stocking?
Natasha Kaplinski, according to an American Express survey.
Probably in stockings.
Meanwhile women don't wish for hubby to be hanging round under the mistletoe.
They'd prefer Sean Connery would pop in for a snog.
What about some Hello pictures of Sean smooching Natasha?
Then we could all be jealous.

STRAIGHTEN HIM OUT

I was livid when I opened my Christmas present from my boyfriend. It was a heavy package, and I couldn't think what it might be.
Imagine how I felt when I pulled the wrapping paper off to find a steam iron inside. Was he trying to tell me something?
Well, I told him something: Find a new girlfriend who doesn't mind being patronised, made a fool of at Christmas, and only aspires to domestic chores.

Martha Mason, Halifax

WHAT'S THIS THEN?

Spare a thought for young Wayne and Coleen, because they face bigger problems than most of us at this time of year; what to buy your loved one for Christmas.

Jewellery? Clothes? A holiday?

Em, they've already had lots of exotic holidays, Coleen's annual clothes bill is reckoned to be in five figures, and once you've both got £10,000 diamond watches, there's only so much left to do in the bling department.

Oh, yeah, and they've got a whole fleet of fancy cars between them.

Perhaps best to give each other money.

Or maybe a book token?

GANTRY GREETINGS

For terrible engineering of seasonal goodwill with business interests, our prize goes to Marples, Ridgeway, Kier, Christiani and Neilsen, the consortium of civil engineers charged with constructing the elevated segment of the M4 motorway west of Chiswick in the early 1960s. They commissioned a painting of their Octopus lifting tackle gantry, and used this for their Christmas Greetings card.

IT'S A BIG ONE

We got this really annoying new boss at work who was appallingly sexist. I don't think he had worked in an environment full of women before (a food packaging factory).

He kept putting his arm round one or other of us and making suggestive remarks. We made it clear we didn't like it but he wouldn't stop.

He then started this thing of asking us what sort or colour of knickers we had on. We didn't laugh it off, we just ignored him.

It was coming up to Christmas so we were preparing our annual party and we knew we'd have to invite him even though none of us wanted to.

We always buy each other little gifts – one person buys one present for one other, then we pull any one out of the box. Having a man in the party would limit the options. So we went ahead as usual with picking presents for each other, then we got this awful black plastic thong with a rubber penis fixed to the front of it from a sex shop. We wrapped this up for our boss.

At our party he opened it up and it really threw him. He couldn't talk and he went really red. We all laughed at him, and really had a go at him. (We'd had a few drinks by then.) It was a complete reversal. He couldn't cope at all.

There was no more mention of knickers or anything else sexual after that, and I'm pleased to say he left the factory a couple of months later.

I hope he reads this and remembers how much he irritated a generally happy group of workers for so long, until we worked out a solution to the problem.

Alice Beamer, Cardiff

A CLASS THING

A Sussex businessman was outraged when he provided his 5-year old daughter with presents to distribute to her friends at school. The teachers confiscated the gifts from the little girl because they had banned Christmas present giving until the last day of term.

Instead of following the complaints procedure, Dad took his woes to the newspapers and told them he went to the Nativity play and saw Jesus get presents. The Head Teacher explained to us that the syndrome could possibly put pressure on other parents to reciprocate, and as there were not gifts for every child in the class, there were dangers of bad feeling being generated.

The Governors of the school had completely backed the Head's decisions, and the matter had now been resolved with the parents.

At the time, the papers reported Dad as saying: "Next they'll be saying you can't let your children wear new shoes because it might upset other parents who can't afford them. Where will it all end?"

WAXING LYRICAL

Madame Tussauds cashed in on Christmas by jacking up a Nativity scene featuring some spare famous faces stuck on the shelves of the waxworks warehouse.

Alphabetically, they'd got a surplus David Beckham, Prime Minister Tony Blair, U.S. President George Bush, Duke of Edinburgh, and Posh Spice.

So what does that give you? Those creative wax manipulators came up with Tony, George and Prince Philip as the Three Wise Men, and Mr and Mrs Beckham as Joseph and Mary.

Inspired?

Well, a Christian traditionalist certainly was – he was inspired to deface the scene – literally – by punching Posh and Becks in the mush, denting their good looks.

SOMEWHAT ACADEMIC

Westbury Homes, the builders, did their seasonal bit to support the public sector in the form of funding an academic study of Christmas tree types.

Professor Ian Stuart-Hamilton of the Department of Developmental Psychology at Glamorgan University was commissioned to analyse the sorts of people who buy particular types of trees.

Plastic ones are the choice of "Quick Fix Kates", whilst pine is picked by "Homebody Heathers".

Either sort will do for "Stylish Suzie" who can make it special with understated decoration and control freak clothing.

Finally "Alternative Amy" won't have a tree but some completely unsuitable decorations that will allow her to celebrate Chinese New Year with crispy duck pancakes.

You know, there could be a masters degree in there somewhere.

FILL HER UP

My son William is a very busy executive for a logistics firm.

Unlike a lot of people he had to work right up to 6 o'clock on Christmas Eve. Nevertheless, he came to visit us on Christmas Day.

However we have our suspicions that he didn't do his Christmas shopping until he was on his way to see us. I got a straw basket full of small pots of marmalade, and his Dad got a spanner set and de-icing kit.

We think he bought these at a petrol station on his way to Manchester from the Midlands.

We didn't say anything, but we're hoping for better next year, William.

Frances Kenton, Cheadle

COLD SHOULDER

Each year a different member of our softball team takes on the task of staging a Christmas party for players and families, old and new. Every year the pressure to make the event memorable and special grows. I was dreading my turn a full twelve months ahead of the date.

When I saw what my predecessor had dreamed up – a World War Two themed evening - complete with tank, I dreaded trying to top that.

I decided to go for something more traditional and dignified. I found out about a guy who did ice sculptures and negotiated with him to get a collection of appropriate centre-pieces for our dining table. I'd invest in some art instead of hiring lots of old uniforms and armaments.

In November the sculptor showed me his designs, and I was impressed. This was going to be a pleasing sight for the gang, and I would be seen as having brought about grace and cultured novelty to the proceedings.

The sculptor was due to deliver the finished works to the restaurant an hour before the guests arrived. He said he'd lend me a nitrogen gun to spray on to the ice to keep it frozen once the pieces were out of their packaging.

A delivery firm brought the sculptures, which looked terrific. Santa in a sleigh, reindeer, trees, presents and a Nativity scene. The guys took off the packaging and left, but forgot to give me the gun. I couldn't track down the sculptor or get a phone call through to the delivery firm, and so the ice started to melt.

By the time guests arrived at the restaurant, all the shape had left the ice structures and they were just like little icebergs sitting on the table surrounded by pools of water.

My efforts proved memorable – but not as planned.

Christian Delavere, Miami

HOW TO PUT IT

"Name name.

Thinking of you at Christmas.

We talk of you still. We haven't forgotten you. And we never will.

If you would like to place a notice in this style, please contact Cynthia."

From the Classified Advertising section of a regional newspaper.

CRAP PRESENT

I always thought my Dad was potty, but when I got a lump of dinosaur dung from him for Christmas, I knew he'd completely lost it.

The stuff is called coprolite – fossilised droppings from prehistoric animals.

Some gift centre in Devon had been passing them off as Christmas presents, and my old man bought it.

David Hatwell, Bristol

BAD BID

Was this book what you wanted for Christmas?

Probably not. Well, you can always join the growing band of people who have graciously received gifts they didn't like the look of, and then have swiftly stuck them up on e-bay in the hope of getting a bit of cash back.

A tyre firm went to the trouble of producing clocks with a picture of a sports car surrounded by a rubber tyre inscribed with good wishes from the manufacturer. One recipient drove this straight to the internet auction site with the description: "This would make any house look crap. Buy it for someone you don't like." Starting price: 1p.

A bank undertook a survey of the syndrome and discovered that the national value of unwanted gifts may be in excess of £1 billion.

XMAS BANDWAGON

Fathers for Justice don't need help when it comes to gaining publicity.

They'll hang off bridges, hurl coloured powders across the House of Commons and wave to the crowds down Pall Mall from the Royal Family's private balcony. If that wasn't enough, a Manchester Bishop suggested fresh tactics to keep them in the public's consciousness.

Reverend Stephen Lowe reckoned the dismissed Dads lobby should jump on the Christmas bandwagon and adopt the New Testament's Joseph as their Saint. But blokes in Batman outfits were not even near the front in a long queue of people and institutions standing by to board the bandwagon…

GLASSY

Readers of the Christmas edition of the Derby Express could take time to study a host of illustrated testimonials for replacement windows across two pages inserted by Trade Windows of Derby to celebrate their twelfth Christmas in business.

The colourful spread included a personal message from the MD: *"Sales figures continue to exceed all our expectations in the face of severe market competition…"* next to an image of a Santa in a sleigh-like JCB manoeuvring a load of – yes, you've got it – replacement windows.

BAA, HUMBUG.

You're an ardent supporter of the Rare Breeds Trust.

Wool from the animals is used to make jumpers by members of the Guild of Spinners, Weavers and Dyers.

How can you get more exposure for their stylish knitting, and raise funds for the charity?

Why by taking pictures of people wearing nothing but the product and turning the shots into a calendar collection.

That was Joan's admirable aim when she arranged for a photographer to snap willing participants completely naked except for a carefully placed sample of knitting.

But hang on. Do the sort of people who buy knitted goods have an appetite for nudity on the wall every month of the year?

Not many, is the answer.

Joan invested £15,000 on producing the calendars. Unfortunately only one in ten found a home.

Nearly 8,000 copies had to be recycled.

And Joan felt a right knit.

THINK CHRISTMAS, THINK PERSIMMON.

The Lichfield Mercury Property supplement set December's mood with decorating know-how tips from "experts" Persimmon Homes, whose Number One recommendation was the subject of Advent Calendars: *"The countdown to Christmas is always an exciting time, especially for the children, so whether you have a chocolate, nativity or home-made calendar, this is an absolute essential to get into the festive spirit."*

And, for the benefit of those torn between the options, the article was generously illustrated with a large colour picture of a child showing sheer delight with her Persimmon advent calendar.

WHAT A FAG

Miss Mistletoe, Miss Reindeer, Mrs Holly and Mrs Santa – an unlikely foursome stepped forth into the streets of Tamworth wielding a giant cigarette. They were the Primary Care Trust Smoking Cessation Team in fancy dress, encouraging residents to give it up for Christmas.

We suspect they made a bigger impact on those who'd been drinking too much.

OUT ON THE TOWN

The Mayor of Uttoxeter chose to devote his Christmas message to praising a local restaurant that is a *"good friend to the town."*

"We would not have achieved our place in next year's national In Bloom finals without its assistance," Geoff Morrison declared.

After a major refurbishment of the premises, the Mayor and his wife performed the re-opening ceremony, in the presence of the junior football team, who had had their kit sponsored by the restaurant.

On the walls inside the improved building were pictures of Uttoxeter streets *"well worth viewing."*

Quite possibly inspired by the restaurant, the Mayor was encouraging people to come up with a logo for the town. He couldn't think of *"a better way to start the New Year than letting everyone know how proud we are of its heritage and how confident we are in its future."*

Our suggestion is a couple of arches inscribed *"We love it."*

Oh, and by the way, the restaurant is called McDonalds.

Yep, that one.

COMMERCIAL BREAK

Our 'Inappropriate Juxtaposition of Imagery' award goes to the designers of the Coca Cola TV ad showing a child magically developing angels' wings and a halo, swiftly followed by a line of 10 juggernauts transporting the fizzy stuff down a dark road in the snow.

BRONZE MEDAL

Our 'Brass-faced Cheek at Cashing in' prize goes to Lichfield's Sun Eleven tanning parlour which ran an ad in mid-December that read: *"Snow should be the only thing that's white this Christmas. Enjoy a flawless Spray Body Tan for just £30. Perfect for Christmas Parties and New Year's Eve."*

GIVE HER THE CHOP

Another runner up in our 'What's it got to do with Christmas?' competition is fitness instructor Catherine Hyde, who managed to get an article in the Worcester Evening News announcing that *"with Christmas and New Year just days away"* it's time to consider your health *"and take up the ancient Chinese martial art Tai Chi."*

EYE-WATERING PR

'Most Unadulterated Reproduction of a Press Release' award goes to Beacon Foods, who got an article headlined: *'They know their onions'* into the Christmas edition of their local paper, without any visible editorial interference. It began: *"Onion products were in demand from award-winning Beacon Foods in the run-up to Christmas as food manufacturers developed new chutneys…"*

Yes, you get the idea.

BOOB

The Daily Star felt their readers needed some uplifting ideas in the Christmas games department, so they suggested finding a couple of pictures of Abi Titmuss and cutting out the bra from one. *"Then pin up the other photo of the babe and blindfold players. See how good they are at sticking the bra in the right place."*

OFF THE BOX

From the seasonal fare on TV we focus on just one bad offering: 'Christmas ruined my life' made by Chrysalis for Channel Five.

The normally impeccably-placed Tony Robinson narrated tales of individual troubles - illustrated by toy angels catching on fire, Santa vomiting and an atomic bomb exploding.

Dramatic reconstructions included a man rubbing his elbow – emotionally capturing the distressing aftermath of a Santa having fallen off a sleigh.

Such tales of woe were interspersed by Bernard Manning in his underpants reading out crap cracker jokes.

Hang on, it all sounds like a TV version of this book.

Perhaps it wasn't so bad after all.

BAD BOOKS

Rather than reading this, perhaps you would have preferred 'Celtic Sex Magic for Couples, Groups and Solitary Practitioners'. That was a Bookseller magazine prize-winning odd title. Other recent annual winners include '227 secrets your snake wants you to know', 'Hot topics in Urology', 'Bombproof your horse' and 'Proceedings from the second international workshop on nude mice, oral sadism and the vegetarian personality'.

Or for more exciting seasonal subject matter, you might want to track down Paul Fanning's 'Christmas Tree Farm Accidents and how to avoid them'.

EARLY START

Way out in front for the 'Tell them pantomime is coming' award has been the Poole Lighthouse Centre for the Arts. Their stylish building was surrounded by huge posters proclaiming the arrival of Brian Cant's version of 'Snow White', due to run from 9th December 2005.

When did the posters first fill the display panels?

Mid July.

PANTS AHEAD

A swanky jewellery shop in Cheshire was displaying an unusual Christmas present prospect – a G-string made with gold and diamonds, priced at £7,000. One window shopper was heard to say: *"If I got one of those, I'd want to wear it on my head, not stuck up my bum."*

JUMPING FOR THE BANDWAGON

So you do dangerous stuff for a living.

No, you're not a postman delivering to both sides of the North Circular Road. You're a professional stunt man.

That means you get paid for risking your life.

But when things are quiet and there's no demand for James Bond stand-ins to undertake death-defying feats, how can you rustle up fresh business?

Send your CV to all the film producers listed in the directories?

Em, yes.

But there's a quicker way to get their attention.

Stick on a Santa suit and ride off the top of Beachy Head on a bike.

Dead easy.

Oh, yes, and wear a parachute that opens when you've reached mid-air.

So – as long as the parachute works properly and the wind doesn't blow you into the cliffs, it's a doddle.

Just drift down towards the rocks below, taking care to avoid the lighthouse coming up unexpectedly between your legs.

Em, have you set a good example for children?

Perhaps not, but surely that phone will ring now that you've appeared in the papers as the Santa who does fake suicides.

"Boss wanted the queue reduced."

THE GOOD OLD DAYS

We've concentrated on recent terrible Christmases, but in case you think it was immensely better in the past, let us point out that there were bad old days too.

DOING IT FOR MONEY

Gifts in a stocking from Santa's visit down the chimney. How on earth did such a notion come about?

The original story of St Nicholas - a Turkish Archbishop - tells of a business-man who went broke and decided he'd have to make his daughters work as prostitutes to keep the wolf from the door, so to speak.

St Nick didn't like the sound of this and so threw little sacks of coins down the man's chimney, which rolled into the girls' stockings, and thus saved them from their fate.

FLAMING HELL

Early American Congressmen aspired to have access to learning. So they began to acquire books and build up a Library. But in 1812 the Brits set fire to it. So the Yanks started again by buying Thomas Jefferson's collection and sticking it in Blodget's Hotel – which didn't sound right.

To improve the image of their endeavours, they invested in a dedicated building and had accumulated 55,000 volumes by Christmas Eve 1851, when another fire broke out accidentally and destroyed more than half the collection.

POOR TRADE

Here's what George Bernard Shaw reckoned to the season in 1893:

"We must be glutinous because it is Christmas. We must be drunken because it is Christmas. We must be insincerely generous; we must buy things that nobody wants, and give them to people we don't like; all because it is Christmas – that is because the mass of the population, including the all-powerful, middle-class tradesman, depends on a week of licence and brigandage, waste and intemperance, to clear off its outstanding liabilities at the end of the year."

OU EST LA GARE?

1910 was not a good year to be aboard a train on Christmas Eve, particularly in France.

A handy website entry for "Disasters at Christmas in the 20th Century" lists all statistics on railway accidents.

Fatal train crashes occurred in England and the USA on 24th December 1910, whilst there were three different accidents on various French lines, followed by a horse-drawn carriage being hit by the Paris Orleans Express on Christmas Day.

WHO'LL DO THE HOOVERING?

President Hoover aimed to make a good impression on those around him during his first Christmas in the White House.

He set up a big dinner party on Christmas Eve 1929. Everyone was focused on entertaining the guests and so no one noticed until it was too late that a fire had started in the West Wing.

In order that party-goers couldn't hear the on-coming fire engines, the ever-resourceful President got the Marine Band to play carols extremely loud until the sirens were turned off.

LOOK - NO PILOT

You're an American bomber pilot assigned to fly a Liberator over Germany on Christmas Day 1944. Nothing critical, but demonstrating to the enemy that you have command of the skies, as ground forces continue to press towards Berlin. Then a German fighter manages to blast off some rounds in your direction, and shells roar into the cockpit, damaging the controls, cutting your oxygen supply and wounding you.

You cannot return this aircraft to England, so time to bail out. You and the flight crew follow procedures to alert the boys in the back, and, leaving the aircraft on autopilot, jump out over Germany with the prospect of spending the rest of the war in a prison camp.

But the Bail Out alarm button was damaged by flak, so the bombardiers further down the fuselage don't know you've left them behind.

They try to talk to you on the intercom but get no answer.

They struggle to peer through to the cockpit, and eventually discover its empty. Oh, dear.

They decide to sit tight until they reckon they're over friendly France.

Then they parachute out of the plane, which continues onward towards England. It flies across the North Sea, passes above the Midlands and eventually runs out of fuel over Herefordshire, crashing on to a farmer's field killing three cows, right in the middle of the King's speech on the radio.

But lots of local kids got extra Christmas presents. They ran to the field and wrenched chunks of the aircraft off as souvenirs.

WHERE SHALL WE STUFF THE FIGS?

"Christmas is the busiest time of year for the family grocer," explained Housewife Consultant Mary Andrews, to her newspaper readers in 1956. *"He wants to give you the best possible service, and here's how you can help him. If you think you will want a bacon joint, order it well in advance. Crackers, tins of biscuits, dates, figs, Dundee cake, all these can be tucked away at home early in December."*

Not like that down the supermarket these days.

DRIVING HIM MAD

You're the Minister of Transport and you've spend the day stuck in the Road Research Laboratory in Slough listening to ways of dealing with traffic problems for the New Year. So an early night prior to Christmas is what you need.

But that wasn't an option for the Right Hon. Ernest Marples in 1959, because some wags had put the word round that there was a free-for-all party at his swanky Westminster apartment, and, in the days before high-security cordons, right through the night various drunken Hooray Henrys kept arriving on his doorstep demanding festive fun and free booze.

He should have stayed overnight at the lab. No-one would have bothered him there.

BIT OF A BLOW

Bored with their presents, as well as 1965 Christmas Day TV, a gang of teenagers in Dade County, U.S.A. climbed into a construction site where contractors were gouging out a drainage canal.

The youths set fire to a storage unit that contained 19.000 pounds of dynamite. The resulting explosion shattered thousands of windows in the nearby town of Homestead, and left unexploded fragments of dynamite scattered across roads and gardens.

GUNNING FOR THEM

Nicolae Ceaucescu and his wife Elena had a Bad Christmas in 1989. The ex-President of Romania and his good lady were shot on Christmas morning by a military firing squad having been found guilty of "crimes against the people".

TRADITIONS AND TASTE

Let's remember the club we've chosen not to join by sniggering at stories of terrible Christmases.

In certain parts it's always a very beautiful thing; perhaps nowhere more so than within the timeless pages of Country Homes and Interiors.

In December 1993, Editor Julia Watson encouraged readers to wire sprigs of gypsophilia among their Christmas tree branches. It's *as delicate as snowflakes, softening the strong green of the fir and the tinny sparkle of the lights."*

Elsewhere in that glistening edition, Jocasta Innes recommended stencilling your present labels with Plaka acrylic, Caroline Charles revealed she was keen on swags of Norwegian pine with cinnamon sticks and tangerines for her Wiltshire cottage, Kim Sisson showed us her lapis lazuli blue flying angels and papier mache balls (rudeness never crossing her mind), and one could invest in Upper Crust crackers containing a broderie anglaise pot pourri sachet.

And all you've got up are some standard issue Woolworths's baubles. Shame.

"Three. Time for the Queen"

BEASTS

Dogs dining on the poinsetta plant, cats chewing through the Christmas tree wiring, hamsters being force fed sweets by next door's children. Such seasonal events led to 17,000 animals making emergency visits to PDSA clinics over Christmas and New Year.

One woman wanted to take her pet turkey along for a check-up, but was worried they might make a meal of it.

Okay, we made that bit up.

GOING ROUND IN CIRCLES

Royal Mail have a Return Letters Department where badly addressed correspondence is opened in order to track down the sender.

One Christmas box without any label contained two live white mice.

NEEDS TRAINING

I bought a dog last summer and my husband, Mark, has had immense pleasure from its delightful company.

We don't have children and openly recognise that Fuzzy, a cross terrier, is a child substitute.

But this was in proportion until Christmas came round.

Mark bought Fuzzy a surprise present. I couldn't think what it was, but it was certainly big and well wrapped.

Mark helped Fuzzy unwrap it on the kitchen floor on Christmas morning.

Inside was a big red railway locomotive, battery-driven. When switched on, it would chuff about on the floor in all directions making a train sound.

Needless to say Fuzzy didn't like it at all.

And I realised I had married a man who was mental.

Tammy Warburton, St Albans

COULDN'T PUT IT DOWN

Different communities, different tastes. Whilst the Marmite recipe book might have been a big 2004 Christmas mover in the Home Counties, best-selling title in the Herefordshire farming town of Bromyard was 'The Encyclopaedia of Chicken Rearing' closely followed by 'Rats and other vermin'.

BAD PUSSY

I scored with a really attractive girl at a Christmas party at a nightclub. She invited me back to her flat. She had two cats, and I'm not a cat person, but I decided to keep my dislike of cats a secret in case that got in the way of what I do like.

After a few drinks, we started to snog on the settee, then we moved to her bedroom. She didn't want to close the bedroom door and the cats were hanging round, but I continued to ignore them.

We started to remove our clothes. I was lying on top of her and started to edge off my underpants. As soon as my bum was bare, one of the cats leapt on it. It freaked me out, and the evening came to an abrupt end.

But she got her claws into me on a later date, so to speak.

Mo Berkeley, East Grinstead

OFF NOTE

We took my mother to the Christmas concert by the Stonnall Singers in our local church - despite the fact she's quite deaf.

When we got there the conductor announced that they had discovered a family of mice had been living inside the piano, so it wasn't in a fit state to function. But the concert would carry on despite the lack of accompaniment.

The choir seemed a little thrown and lost it a few times, which was disappointing for everyone - apart from my mother who was oblivious to these shortcomings and enjoyed every moment of it.

Melinda Read

CRUNCH TIME

Rosy Greaves decided to auction a cornflake on e-bay.

No hoper? Not likely.

She got 300 hits in an hour and saw the bids reach £51.

Why? It was in aid of a charity – The Dogs Trust.

Then the e-bay administrators stepped in and closed down her auction.

We don't do foodstuffs, they explained.

UP THE WRONG TREE

Our neighbours stuck a row of horrible twinkling electric reindeer across their front lawn, and our dog, Miles, got really upset.

He wouldn't stop barking when we walked him – day or night. So we had to put him in the car with a blanket over his head and get him out of the street before he could have his walk.

We rang the RSPCA, but they said "such a phenomena wasn't their mandate to tackle."

Zena Tookay, Chiswick

TALKING TURKEY

Here's to the Inland Revenue.

There's a tax exemption on business Christmas parties of up to £150 per head. This covers all costs including any transport and accommodation including VAT. So you could get a taxi to a room in, say, a Holiday Inn and maybe have enough left over for a half of lager.

That's good, isn't it!

However the event must be open to all staff on similar terms.

Yes, none of your *"only those in the accounts department can go, and we'll leave out that fat bloke who scoffs all the scampi, then farts over the vol au vents"*.

PriceWaterhouseCoopers explained to business bosses that they must be beware of flu epidemics which could decimate numbers and thus take the average over £150, in which case the well-intentioned event becomes tax liable. Yeah, get them there with a few Beechams powders forced down their throats if necessary rather than finding yourself having to cough up for the Chancellor's coffers.

Another vital point to bear in mind during the season of goodwill: don't give anyone a turkey as the inspectors may not class this as a trivial benefit and might demand tax on the cost of providing a turkey over the previous six years, even though you did it only once.

In short, tread carefully, otherwise the Exchequer will take the shine off your tinsel.

NOT IN THE BROCHURE

Visit a winter wonderland for a trip to remember. That's what it said in the advertising literature, so Frances Middleton was delighted when her brother was able to make this dream come true and took her off to Lapland.

What about a reindeer-drawn sleigh ride in the snow?

Sounded like the icing on the cake.

And it was, until the sleigh turned over, tipping Frances out on to the snow.

Then the next sleigh following behind didn't stop, but carried on and ran over her leg, breaking her ankle – making it more of a holiday to remember than she'd ever expected.

Frances, who was working at the time as an assistant retail manager, was off work for seven weeks with her leg in plaster.

And those reindeer seem so sweet.

GAME FOR A LAUGH

To maximise profits, commercial estates snare, trap, shoot and poison millions of mammals and birds of prey every year.

And now the commercial shooting industry wants us to put its waste products – gamebird corpses – on our plates.

Supermarkets are stocking pheasant and partridge as some sort of "wild" or "natural" alternative to factory farmed meat.

We have investigated overcrowding and neglect suffered by tens of millions of these birds bred to supply commercial shooting estates.

To prevent pecking and cannibalisation, chicks have plastic 'bits' inserted into their nostrils.

Their wings are clipped before they are crammed into crates and shipped to the estates where wealthy customers will pay thousands of pounds to spend a day blasting them out of the sky.

Douglas Batchelor, League Against Cruel Sports

ABOUT RAT

The Keep Britain Tidy boss blamed louts abandoning fast food containers for increasing the rat population.

Because street sweepers work less shifts over Christmas the quantities of kebab, pizza, chip and burger wrappings in the gutter mounts dramatically.

That in turn encourages brown rats to emerge from sewers to enjoy a seasonal feast.

KBT executive Alan Woods declared: "This is a recipe for a rat plaque the likes of which we haven't seen for years."

BAD TURKEY

Let's not dwell on how turkeys are becoming bigger year on year. (Though it's generally unlikely to be through their enjoyment of the outdoors and a range of natural foodstuffs.)

But in the last ten years, the typical Christmas turkey has gone from weighing in at 9 kilos to something in the region of thirteen.

And that's unlucky for the ovens, because they're not really comfortable with such demanding occupants.

Some domestic ovens - that see little other than instant dinners for most of the year - are suddenly put to the test on Christmas Day when Mum jams that massive bird through the door.

And some ovens don't like it, as British Gas service engineers discovered.

They had their worst ever Christmas Day call out in 2004.

Over 600 emergencies as a result of those big birds spilling fat into the machinery, which started a fire or blew the micro-chip controls.

And there's nothing worse that a dead turkey in a dead oven.

WHAT'S ON THE TREE FOR ME?

We came home from a day's Christmas shopping to discover our dog Little Bro had attacked the Christmas tree.

We'd put some chocolate novelties on the branches and he'd obviously smelt them and so jumped up to get at them.

The tree was at an angle, so he'd been pulling hard at the branches. There were also broken glass baubles on the carpet and so we reckoned he might have bitten into them as well as the foil-covered chocolate.

We took him to the vets and had him x-rayed and the vet told us there were fragments of the bauble in his stomach.

They might pass through him without harming him, but there was a chance the sharp edges could pierce his intestines. So we agreed for Little Bro to have an operation, which cost £285.

Our precious pet had taken a big bite out of our Christmas spending money.

Victoria McCrick, Huddersfield

BED GIVEAWAY

My husband George and I were invited to stay with my sister's family for Christmas, arriving on Christmas Eve and staying over until Boxing Day.

My sister, Carole, is not keen on dogs, but they agreed that we could bring our poodle, Bundle, providing he would sleep in the car at night.

We agreed to this and arrived and enjoyed a pleasant Christmas Eve with our relatives. Their children liked Bundle and kept giving him Quality Street chocolates despite us telling them that chocolate is bad for dogs.

With reluctance we put Bundle into our car for the night. I was very worried about him suffering from the cold out there.

I couldn't sleep because of my anxiety, so George went down to the car and sneaked Bundle into the house and up to our bedroom.

Bundle and I were delighted, and the little chap (by which I mean the dog) settled down on top of the duvet (as he generally did at home) and all three of us were able to relax.

Early in the morning my husband woke me. It seemed much too early for adults to exchange presents, but in fact he was alerting me to the present Bundle had given us.

Our little dog had suffered diarrhoea - doubtless due to the chocolate - and had left a very nasty mess in the middle of the duvet, and it had soaked well in. We felt terrible, particularly as we had gone against Carole's wishes by allowing him into the bedroom.

George sneaked Bundle back out to the car as I looked in horror at the mess. Should I tell my sister what had happened, or try to repair the damage?

Not wanting to spoil their Christmas Day, I decided discretion was the best way forward.

I took a shower – with the duvet and cover, and spent ages in there trying to get the mess and the marks off the material and from inside the duvet itself. It was a start, but far from satisfactory.

Thankfully Bundle didn't have any recurrence of his problem in the car.

That night the poor little chap did have to sleep in the car, whilst George and

I tried to avoid the damp patches in the bed caused by the wet duvet.

On Boxing Day morning we declared we would take the bed linen home and launder it and return it.

Carole gave us very dirty looks, but let us remove the duvet from the house. We were able to get the stain out of the cover, but the duvet itself was beyond hope. We spent several days in the sales trying to find a perfect replacement, and eventually we bought a high quality duvet and arranged to have that sent to my sister's address, saying her duvet had been damaged at the dry cleaners. This all happened five years ago, and Carole never pressed me to explain what went on over that Christmas holiday.

I wrote this and showed it to her, and she told me that her husband had seen George take Bundle from the car at midnight on Christmas Eve, and they'd figured out we'd had a little accident.

Jean Parsons, Basildon

"What's next-door-but-one's budgie called?"

RELATIVELY PAINFUL

A Dickensian Christmas was different.

It was not all about buying, swopping (then selling on e-bay) ship loads of Chinese junk.

More about fattening up a goose rather than the regular gruel.

A few songs round the fire and a thimble of sherry.

Not Grand Auto Theft update and 10 cans of Stella.

So we should be understanding upon encountering Charles Dickens's syrupy enthusiasm:

"Who can be insensible to the outpourings of good feeling, and the honest interchange of affectionate attachment which abound at this season of the year. A Christmas family-party. We know nothing in nature more delightful."

He obviously never had his Grannie make a gruesome mess in the toilet.

BIT OF A KNEES UP

The first Christmas I went to my husband's family home in Newcastle we were taken down the pub one evening to meet Uncle Harold who had served in the Second World War in the army and had lost his arm in battle.

He had a false arm with a false hand on the end of it, and I remember it gave me the creeps when I shook hands with him.

Then things got worse. I sat next to him in the pub, and as the evening wore on, his arm drifted towards me and his false hand settled on my knee. He seemed completely unaware of this, and I nudged his hand away.

I started to imagine he was doing this deliberately.

I had to knock his arm away three or four times that evening. The last time I gave it a strong shove to make the point, and he turned round and said he could take it off if it was annoying me.

Sheila Govern, Leicester

THE NUMBERS GAME

My father is often a big challenge to us on Christmas Day. Since my mother died, he has looked to us to provide him with a satisfactory Christmas, and often we are made to feel we have not done enough to support and entertainment him. But last year he announced that he didn't want to see anyone until lunchtime on Christmas Day.

He'd find ways of amusing himself.

This was a blessing.

When we went round to collect him to bring him to our house for Christmas lunch, he showed us how he'd spent the morning.

He'd cut out a grid from the newspaper the previous day and had been tackling Suduko for the first time. He'd spend two hours at it, but hadn't got very far.

We looked at the grid which was much wider than the normal 9 by 9 box, and realised that it was a bingo card which he'd been trying to fill in.

Sheila Pears, Stratford

PROPPING UP THE PASTE TABLE

Guess what I got on Christmas Eve? A big candle in the shape of a penis.
Tasteless? Maybe, but fun. My husband and I lit it and drank champagne.
Well, after 23 years of wedded bliss, you need to come up with something novel.
The first dribbles of wax from the melted top slightly disguised the thing, so we left it on the table for our Christmas lunch, and when Granny and Aunt Ethel came round they didn't spot the true nature of this decoration.
My turkey was too dry, gravy too lumpy and carrots too mushy, but apart from that it was a pretty good meal – laid out on the paste table, as our dining table was too small.
Aunt Ethel spent the afternoon farting loudly whilst the rest of us played charades.
I suppose I could have shut her up with that candle, but Goodwill to all women and what have you.

Elizabeth Hayden-Jones, Worcester

SEEING THE WRONG THING

We were due to go to my Aunt Debbie's on Christmas Day.
Mum had warned my brother and I that Auntie had a friend who was blind who might be there.
When we got to the house we were introduced to Patsy, who was wearing very thick specs. We took this to be the blind person and spent the day passing things to her and pointing out things to her.
She seemed very grateful and we were very impressed at how confidently she was able to deal with things in a strange house where she couldn't see anything.
We were watching, and Patsy was listening to, the Queen's speech when Patsy suddenly said: "Oh, look, it's starting to rain."
We realised that Patsy wasn't blind at all.
My brother and I began to laugh and the rest of the family demanded to know what we were laughing at.
Thankfully everyone saw the funny side, including Patsy.
And Auntie later told her blind friend who thought it was hilarious.

Megan Deal, Richmond

LOUNGE LIZARD

My daughter, Charlotte, wanted her boyfriend, Julian, to come and stay with us over Christmas. I was a bit wary but agreed, as Charlotte convinced me he was potentially Mr. Right.
Then she asked if his father could come too. Julian's Dad had been recently widowed and was at a loose end.
I wasn't particularly happy about this prospect but felt I couldn't just leave him out if he was potentially going to be the grandfather of my daughter's children.
So Julian and his father turned up on Christmas Eve.
The man spooked me from the moment he arrived. He conveyed a sense of lust, directed at both Charlotte and me. He dressed like a lounge lizard and had horrible hair that seemed dyed a sort of pink shade to disguise natural ginger. He kept touching us in a very cosy manner, as if he were our life long friends.
I told Charlotte to tell Julian to tell him to back off.
Julian took his Dad down to the pub, and when they came back the old man seemed a little more subdued, thank goodness.
I thought everything was going to work out all right, but after supper, when I'd

finished in the kitchen, I went upstairs and discovered Julian's Dad in my bedroom exploring my underwear drawer.

Charlotte and I kicked them both out that evening.

That dirty old man did not become the grandfather of my grand children.

Maggie Portington, Hatfield

TERRIBLY SORRY, IT FELL OFF THE LORRY

Dozens of poets wanted to platform their rhymes in our pages, but it's not that sort of book. However to demonstrating we're not completely dismissive of the art, we take pleasure in offering a brief extract from Jenni Doherty's lovely 'Saving Christmas Past':

"The Christmas I was lost in the blur of hurried kisses from anyone and everyone in enormous rooms and carolled corners with old adversaries, old best friends, old flames, old fools. The shake, the rattle and the Barcardi rum – mingling and jingling with the thrills and spills of seasonal love… Brotherly love, divine love, Christian love, drunken love. Love thy neighbour, love thy postman, love the brother's girlfriends' cousin…"

STIFF UPPER LIP

A family down the road from us had a bereavement just before Christmas. No one could have been more sympathetic than us that these nice people had lost their Grandma just before the festive season.

To add to their woes, they were told that the funeral couldn't be until two days after Boxing Day. But then a neighbour told us the family decided to have their Grandma in the house over Christmas.

We couldn't believe it.

They got the funeral director to bring the body in its coffin back to the house on Christmas Eve. I watched this in horror from our front room, and wasn't the only neighbour to find this prospect ghastly.

I was told afterwards that they had the old lady lying with them whilst they watched TV, and they pretended to let her join in some card games.

Thank goodness we hadn't known about that at the time. The whole thing freaked us out as it was.

We were trying to entertain our family, whilst down the road they had a dead body as the special guest. Spooky.

Joanna Smith, Wiltshire

SHORT CUT

My fiercely independent elderly mother spent last Christmas in hospital suffering from burns after she'd tried to heat mince pies in her electric toaster, then endeavoured to extract the charred bits with her bare fingers without pulling out the plug.

This year she'll be staying with us.

David Bartholomew, Leicester

ONE FOR THE DIARY

My late father, Thomas Mayhew, was a wonderful man, who worked diligently as a tax inspector all his life. He had lots of hobbies and interests, and a few bees in his bonnet, one of which related to Christmas.

He got it into his head that life would be easier if Christmas Day fell on the same day of the week every year. The trigger for such a notion came from some complicated aspect of the Christmas holidays that impacted on the way tax was calculated.

My father concluded that the world would be a better place (at least for Her Majesty's Inspectors of Taxes) if Christmas Day could always be a Thursday, to be followed by Boxing Day on a Friday. Normal working hours would come to an end on Christmas Eve afternoon (the Wednesday), and the following Monday could be the start of another short working week.

His means of adjusting the days to bring this about required adding or subtracting to the number of days in November, in order that the First of December always fell on a Monday. That adjustment would then be balanced out at the end of January, which would be allocated more or less days as necessary to allow February to commence at the appropriate point in the Gregorian calendar.

I've got a file of correspondence on my father's obsession, including letters to several Prime Ministers and Chancellors of the Exchequer. Bless him.

Tara MacIntosh, Edinburgh

WARM ENOUGH NOW FOR YOU?

My mother came to stay with us for Christmas. Despite having the central heating on all day, she kept complaining she felt cold.

My husband had to go back to her flat and bring over her trusty old electric fire. Except it wasn't trusty.

Grannie insisted on having it in her room. I kept telling her there wasn't enough space, but she assured us she'd be careful.

The rest of us were watching TV when we heard the screams. She'd got the fire too close to the duvet and had set the bed alight.

Mercifully she wasn't injured.

We got her out of the room, which stank of smoke.

She slept in our room, and my husband and I had to sleep on the floor downstairs.

All Boxing Day, Grannie complained about being too warm.

Old people, don't you love them!

Maggie McFarlane, Cheltenham

NOT SO GREAT, NOT SO GOOD

For most of us, mercifully, the hell of Christmas is a private matter, but others must blunder through the horrors of it all in the middle of a very public platform…

CELL OUT
You are the undisputed Queen of kitchen prowess. Superwoman of home making.
You've delighted millions of people with your unrivalled Christmas decoration making talents displayed on television.
Then, due to an irritating misunderstanding over share dealing, it turns out you've violated some ridiculous federal law – and so you're sent to jail.
Well, the opportunities to show off your domestic magic are somewhat limited here.
But then a competition is announced – to make a Christmas decoration in jail.
Ah, a challenge, an audience, the opportunity to triumph, albeit only amongst a gang of old lags.
You rustle something up – and bugger me, if you're not picked as the winner.
Well, these judges are no better than those on the outside.
Biased bastards.

CONGRATULATIONS
Cliff Richard treated his team of office flunkies to a Christmas night out, naturally.
He took them all to a Chinese restaurant.
And guess what?
There just happened to be a karaoke machine in one corner.
So, never one not to join in the spirit of things, Cliff stepped up to the mic, and did a turn.
Apparently no-one else in the restaurant took any notice of him.
Must have been a strange experience.

OFF SIDE
The Leicester City football team Christmas party in a night club was suddenly stopped mid-game when a squad of drugs officers arrived and demanded that everyone freeze whilst the toilets were searched.
For fifteen minutes the lads hung round bemoaning their fate at being on the receiving end of unwanted press attention.
Eventually the drug busters emerged from the lav and sounded an all clear.
The Leicester fun-lovers were left to continue with their innocent knees-up, wondering if they had been the victim of a malicious whistle-blower.

GOLDEN OLDIE
You're a topless dancer, doing your stuff in a Houston strip club. Your surgically enhanced bosom is working well, drawing the male crowds round your pole.
One of them's an old geezer, who really takes a fancy to you.
Well, that's understandable.
He's no hunk, but it turns out he's loaded in other ways.
Blow me, if he's not some doddery old millionaire.
If you can put up with his pawing, you might get your hands on a heap of his cash.

So you agree to go on a date with the fragile old fella.

The man's almost ninety, and looks like a skeleton with skin stretched over it.

You're just twenty and gorgeous enough to get featured in Playboy magazine.

Naturally, the two of you make a lovely couple.

You're flattered when the old man asks to marry you. How could you refuse? He's got $60 million in the bank.

So the arrangements are made, and you make your vows. Each will look after the other in sickness and in health.

No prizes for guessing who'd need the better bedside manner.

Yes, he lasted just 14 months, then Anna Smith was left alone with the family fortune.

We can only imagine how distraught she must have been.

But then along came Pierce Marshall, the millionaire's son, who reckoned Dad would have wanted him to have all the dosh.

A string of expensive law cases later, and poor little Anna discovers her Christmas present is no more than the miserable $5 million in gifts from hubby. Heart-breaking.

BATMAS

What does Batman do for Christmas? Why turn up at a burger van in Canterbury for an early snack.

And who should he bump into there?

Why, none other than Spiderman and Superman.

Wouldn't you have thought the three super-heroes could have exchanged cards and presents on this seasonal occasion?

No – blows.

The fancy dress participants on their way home from a big party fell out and had to be separated by Kent police officers before they made mincemeat of each other.

CUT THE CARDS

If you dread the task of doing Christmas cards to all your friends, spare a thought for Tony Blair, because he's got more friends than you've even dreamt of.

Tory David Davis invested a precious Parliamentary question in asking Number Ten how many cards would the Prime Minister be posting.

1,900 was the reply.

"And how much will that cost the nation?" demanded the fearless opposition front-bencher.

£405, explained a Downing Street spokesperson.

Em, that wouldn't cover the cost of second class stamps, so we must assume the postage element was met from another budget.

But it does reveal that Tony's using cards that cost just 21p each.

Perhaps those ones they sell off in Woolworths in January?

BACK TO THE BAR

A barrister was disbarred by the Bar Council just before Christmas.

How unseasonal of them.

However, they were dealing with a man who had taken on a murder case at the Old Bailey, and then ambitiously agreed to handle another murder case up in Stafford, which meant he was not always available in either court room (stuck on Intercity trains most days), and was a little behind with his briefs, to say the least.

Oh yes, and at the same time he was on bail over two allegations of sexual assault in his own "private life".

On top of that, it was alleged he was supplying someone with class A drugs. As luck would have it, he was also found guilty of having wasted the court's time over the preparation of evidence.

(Could this be helped when he had so much on his plate?)

One other thing: he was declared bankrupt around this time.

Okay, a Bad Christmas, but, all in all, looking forward to the New Year.

I mean, what's diminishing "public confidence in the legal profession and bringing it into disrepute" amongst friends?

IT'S THE THOUGHT THAT COUNTS

And so the young couple took a room at the estate, and thereupon a star lit up the sky, and three wise men came to worship the children. They were: from the south, Arun Nayar; from the east, Sven-Goran Eriksson; and from the west, Greg Rusedski.

Hang on, hang on – who's that Arun bloke?

Only the very lucky man dating Liz Hurley; for she was there too, almost angel-like in her grace and… well, angelic qualities.

Oh yeah, and Sven brought his bird along, naughty Nancy – perhaps not quite first-in-the-field regards the silvery wings department.

Come on, what's this all about?

Why, the Beckhams's babies' christening ceremony – staged in a specially-built shed done up as a pretend chapel round the side of their massive Hertfordshire mansion just before Christmas.

Brooklyn and Romeo were being blessed, with Elton John shining down upon them.

And David and Victoria shipped in the Bishop of Cork to do the business; thus upsetting the local clergy, who were at pains to point out they hadn't seen much of the celebrated stars down the local church, and unless the shed had been appropriately consecrated, the event may not have been a valid christening.

GETTING THEIR KICKS

I saw Manchester United twice on Saturday 18th December 2004. In the afternoon I was a heart-warmed spectator at the ground when the boys thrashed Crystal Palace 5 – 2.

Imagine my surprise when late that evening I went to a club in Manchester with two mates and saw most of the team that had played that afternoon done up in smart suits having a bit of a Christmas do.

And there were more incidents here than there had been on the pitch.

I reckon a lot of the people in the Man United party, if not the players themselves, had had a skinful. There were certainly a couple of scuffles which a ref would have jumped on.

Dick Markhan, Eccles

WRONG LANE

You're President of the Institute of Advanced Motorists and you've got nine points on your licence. Do you drive carefully?

Well, not that carefully – because you are also a Member of the Royal Family.

Oh, yes?

His Royal Highness the Duke of Gloucester, no less. Cousin to the Queen.

So you can look forward to a bit of leniency from the coppers, can you?

Apparently not.

You do 70 mph on a 60 mph stretch and you end up before the beak.

Surely there are extenuating circumstances?

Unfortunately the Duke couldn't think of any.

So a 12-point ban was immediately brought into effect. The great man had to hand his licence over to the court usher and make other arrangements rather than motoring home the day before Christmas Eve.

Mercifully, living at Kensington Palace, he's handy to Harrods for any last minute shopping

Perhaps he could wrap up the car - now he doesn't need it - and give it to one of the servants?

As for the Presidency of the Institute – perhaps he's not the best role model for next year.

TITANIC STRUGGLE

Feel, if you will, for movie star Kate Winslett and her devilishly handsome director husband Sam Mendes.

The couple worked immensely hard to prepare their new home in time for Christmas last year.

Alas, those lazy good-for-nothing builders didn't knuckle down to the tasks in hand. And instead were probably up the pub sinking a pint or three.

So Kate and Sam had to spend Christmas Day in an outhouse.

Now, your idea of an outhouse might be a small shed full of spiders and old tins of paint where you keep the bikes and lawnmower, but the Mendes family have 22 Cotswold acres to inhabit, so we reckon their concept of outhouse ain't what we'd call roughing it.

THE FUTURE'S ORANGE?

After Mark Thatcher admitted involvement in preparations for the overthrow of a government regime, letter writers to the Guardian newspaper made it clear they assumed the ex-Prime Minister's son would be treated like all other parties guilty of subversion and would be taken by the Americans to Guantenamo Bay for further questioning, to spend Christmas in an orange suit in a cage with a prayer mat for company.

DEFENSIVE PLAY

Gosh, there's Robin Hood swigging from a bottle of spirits.

Oh, okay then, it's actually West Brom footballer Bernt Haas in fancy dress at his Christmas party.

You see, he's Swiss and stuck in the Midlands, so he doesn't know any better.

But he's drinking rather a lot.

He got in such a state that his relatively sober pals called an ambulance and had him taken into hospital where staff were able to show the sloshed Alp-hugger what he needed to do in order to stand up without artificial aids.

Let's hope he was feeling much better by the time the Albion were due to play their Boxing Day fixture at home to Liverpool.

The result? The Baggies lost five nil.

Bugger the Hawthornes, back to the booze, perhaps?

SLIPPERY SOAP

One Christmas you're a big star in East Enders, with girls in nightclubs falling at your feet. Next year you're a wishy washy Aladdin... no, that's wrong. You're Wishy Washy in Aladdin at a Southsea theatre.

Not great, but better than a poke in the eye with a sharp stick.

You're going to do the decent thing on Christmas Day and spend it at home with the family, then it's back to Southsea for your Boxing Day matinee.

Sounds fine, but those relatives come round. Yeah, the rough ones, who drink too much. And, after a few bevies, tempers fray and rude things get said about your career, behaviour, looks, whatever.

Big row, big fight, big police officers come round to sort out the mess.

"Haven't we seen you on TV, sir?"

"Not recently."

The ex-East Enders star gets dragged off to the station, but after questioning he was released on bail, so he could scurry down to Southsea in time for the "He's behind you!" routine.

ACTING UP

Blender magazine produced a Christmas survey of worst examples of rock stars attempting to act.

Top spot went to Madonna, whom they reckoned *"adopts a glassy-eyed expression of someone on drugs, and delivers lines like she's reading out poison pen letters."*

WINNER EVERY TIME

Film director Michael Winner added another trophy to his bulging cabinet in the form of starring in the most irritating TV commercial of 2004: the Esure insurance "I'm not his sister" campaign.

He joins Billy Connolly who didn't get a lot of laughs for his National Lottery ad in the Marketing magazine's annual awards.

As there is no rule saying you can't win twice in a row, having seen a few of his recent television campaigns, some people reckon Michael's in with a chance for the double.

DANDY MANDY

We don't know how Peter Mandleson spent Boxing Day last year, but we're sure it won't have been chuckling amiably at the 1978 picture of him, that one paper dug out, when he was a delegate to a Cuban political conference.

He's shown wearing dodgy sandals, dodgy flared trousers, dodgy T-shirt and dodgy beard.

In summary, dodgy all over, clapping his hands with delight next to a gorgeous young Cuban woman who's acting as hostess for the party of radical Brits.

MAYOR IN CHAINS

You're a senior citizen who has served the community man and boy. Now you hold a titular office – as Mayor for a year.

What does it involve? Not much more than a few beers at a few functions, the odd speech, and swinging that gold chain about to prove who you are.

Well, one old St Albans's Mayor got the hang of it, then hit a bad patch.

First of all he lost the chain of office. In a bar, where he'd been functioning extremely well up until that point.

Then next night it was off to the local panto, and he couldn't help but notice the glamorous waitress serving the drinks in the interval.

In best Mayoral tradition, he grabbed hold of her and asked for a couple of jugs.

The young lady got all flushed.

And next day the talk of the Town Hall was that the good-spirited civic functionary had let down the chain of office.

CHERIE ON THE ICING

One of the secrets of successful publishing is to correctly estimate the likely sales of your end product, so you produce the appropriate number in your print run, and thus minimise costs and maximise return.

Very hard to get right, and easy to be out by a few thousand copies one way or another (as we know to our cost).

But you've got a very famous lady, seldom not in the news. And she's written about all sorts of interesting things, not least life at 10 Downing Street as wife of the Prime Minister.

Well, that's a sure fire winner, no worries.

You can confidently go with a print run of 100,000. After all, half a million people bought Lynn Truss's little study of punctuation.

So, good launch on Richard and Judy. Lots of press coverage, and the copies are in view in every bookshop in the land.

But come year end and it seems your estimates were a bit out.

In fact, you wish you'd taken a nought off that initial figure.

At one point, there were more than 90,000 copies hanging round the warehouse.

LESS TO SMILE ABOUT

Just before Christmas I was pleased to see that Axa Sun Life Insurance got a present from the Financial Services Authority – a £500,000 fine for running misleading advertisements featuring Carol Smillie.

I was one of the mugs who had been shelling out for a dodgy endowment policy.

I'm sure she knew nothing about the shenanigans, but in future let's hope the smiling star of all those TV make-over shows will stick to slapping wallpaper on people's living rooms, where the damage is generally just short term.

David Alexander, Guildford

GONGS FOR GAFFES

The Conservative party put a big question mark against some of the Labour governments recipients of New Year honours last year.

They pointed out the Permanent Secretary at the Home Office was knighted just days after a report announced civil servants couldn't remember what had happened over events when David Blunkett had been seeking to fast track a visa for Kimberly Quinn's nanny.

Richard Bowker, who stepped down as the Head of the Strategic Rail Authority, got a CBE after it was announced the quango he'd been running would be abolished because it didn't work.

And the "retiring" boss of the disastrously mal-functioning Child Support Agency, Doug Smith, picked up a Commander of the Order of the Bath, when many thought he should have been thrown out with the bathwater.

SOGGY HOGGY

You're a parliamentary columnist for a broadsheet newspaper. You're a wine correspondent for a political weekly. You're the presenter of a radio satire show about the week's news. What could be better?

Well, you could do a book full of those round robin letters that some people send out with their Christmas cards and make a seasonal killing.

And you could have a fling with a wild American bird who puts it about a bit and hope your wife won't find out.

All was looking simply divine for Simon (whose old Dad Richard was a seminal socialist from up north made good by writing about Literacy in the 1950s).

But then things started to unravel.

Hoggo was having it off with the woman who was 'seeing' a Cabinet Minister, but who decided to get married, and claim her children belonged to her new husband.

Okay, thinks Hoggy. Keep your head down. No need for this to flare up in my direction.

But that damned Secretary of State – another socialist from up north – gets all girly about his rights of access to the kid. The bastard is pursuing paternal petitions through the courts, and the News of the World has told its readers.

Let's hope this story doesn't turn up on 'The News Quiz', thinks Hoggy. If it does, should I use my chairman's prerogative to drop it as being extremely unfunny?

And so the great man gets on with sniggering at politicians in his newspaper column, jeering at others' misfortunes on the satire show.

He uses the Guardian to plug his Christmas book. Cheap laughs at the expense of letters written in innocence and good faith by others. How hilarious, and what a perfect stocking filler.

But, oh dear. The Blunky/Kimbo battle is breaking out into the open on all fronts.

The peeved politician is claiming he could be a Dad.

When might all this have been conceived?

Oh, dear. That week.

Our hero sensibly huddles in a quiet corner. It would be just too awful if the spotlight drifted in his direction. After all, he didn't even really… Well, let's not get into the tacky details.

There's nothing to connect him to that troublesome woman, is there?

Apart from the nasty accusations dodgy Dave made to him about hanging around his beloved bird far too much. Thank goodness no-one was looking. Only the guide dog could see the wine buff wobbling.

On the Saturday before Christmas a journalist calls. What might this be? More publicity for his scoffing remarks about other people's Christmas letters?

Nope. A scoundrel from the tabloids is accusing the man of letters of having been Kimberly's other other lover. What? The third man.

How scandalous. How outrageous. What nonsense, says Simon, simply.

But we know for a fact, say the hacks, now braying at his door.

Oooooh, dear.

Em, it was like this. She and I were friends, but I never had sex with her.

Oh yes you did. And we can prove it.

Em, well, "contrary to the impression I gave last night we did have a sexual relationship, which started before her marriage, but the relationship became very infrequent indeed afterwards."

Very infrequent indeed. That should play well at Hogg Towers.

Or was the great man about to have a crap Christmas? And what would the New Year hold in store?

Could he continue hosting the 'News Quiz'? he wondered. Angus Deayton didn't survive his shenanigans to stay on 'Have I got News for You'. Will the BBC bosses be forgiving under the circumstances?

After all, it was very infrequent indeed, once she was married.

(Would Mrs H be wondering if the 'infrequent' was out of mutual choice, or simply a reflection of Kimby not being quite so available as in the past?

What must Hoggy's poor old Dad have made of it all? The boy went soft down south trying to score with stuck-up slappers, and his uses of literacy became no more than cobbling together the seasonal correspondence of others.)

Talk about brass-faced. Day after the debacle, Hog's back in the Commons gazing down from the Lobby at poor old Blunky – now back on the back benches - and snearing at the elected members.

Well, at least he wouldn't have to suffer that horrible business of eye-contact in the corridors of power with his competing suitor for Mrs Thingy's affections, or the results of them at least.

He could pass his amorous rival without having to turn his eyes to the ground. Praying the dog wouldn't smell sweat in the air and give him a nasty bite in the Ball and Trumpet.

"Where have you been? You've got mince pie between your teeth and you stink of sherry."

THE LONGEST DAY

The end results of many a Bad Christmas take place in the vicinity of the toilet, but we'll spare you the gory details as generously supplied by a flush of would-be correspondents.

Suffice it to say that in households where one lavatory works just fine on 364 days of the year, after excess consumption, heavy drinking, chocolate gorging and sundry other indulgence, the demands on the facility by the extended family can steadily become overwhelmed.

We would like to hereby recommend a cloakroom ticket system (like they have on the deli counter at Waitrose) whereby you take a ticket to show your place in line, and lowest number gets inside next.

This needs to be policed, as the unscrupulous may be inclined to plan ahead and take more than one ticket from the strip.

In the event of disputes or desperation, it will be judicious to place a bucket in the back yard.

Those in flats may find carrier bags a blessing at such dire times.

But please do not throw these out of the window.

WHEN IN ITALY

As a Christmas treat for my girlfriend, I booked us a flight to Milan and arranged accommodation at a small hotel in Bergamo.

The plane landed early afternoon on Christmas Eve, and we wasted about two hours trying to work out how to get to Bergamo by public transport, which was all on the brink of shutting down that afternoon.

We eventually took a taxi that got us to the hotel around 6 o'clock.

It turned out we were the only people staying there over Christmas, and the owner couldn't wait for us to check in so he could leave himself.

We asked him about food on Christmas Day and Boxing Day. He told us to go the shops and we could use the kitchen.

We hurried off to the shops but they had all closed. We got some snacks and chocolate from a garage, and returned to the hotel.

The kitchen was more or less bare, but we did find where the wine was kept.

We now discovered that the heating was off, and we couldn't see how to turn it on, and it was freezing.

The proprietor had left us a phone number to reach him on, but he didn't answer any of our calls.

On Christmas Day we went to all the other hotels in the town in the hope that they could feed us, but none could fit us in, so we returned to our hotel and got back into bed with crisps, chocolate and wine.

And watched Italian TV for the rest of the day.

Richard Beacham, Hastings

LATE PRESENT

Christmas Day and you've had two and half times the legal limit for alcohol whilst driving, but you reckon you can get home in one piece without anyone noticing. Just find your way through Hounslow slowly and carefully.

But that wasn't how it looked to other people, who were sure there was a drunk at the wheel.

They alerted the police who pursued the "erratic" car and stopped it. The lady driver came up with a novel excuse. She'd been attending a funeral.

On Christmas Day? Feltham magistrates didn't buy it. She got a £300 fine and a 2 year ban.

SHORT OF SATISFACTION
The consumer society has stimulated us to pillage the planet to pursue our every whim.

The modern media quickly turn innocent children into dissatisfied little monsters whose daily real life experiences seem inconsequential in comparison to the riches and variety of the screen worlds to which they have been mindlessly exposed.

We spend a fortune indulging them on Christmas Day, and swiftly they are dissatisfied once more, and are seeking further novelty.

You can see why illicit drug taking's caught on.

George Berkeley, Bucks.

TURKEY AGAIN
A man from Wiltshire reckons he's consumed more than 5,000 turkeys.

He's a Christmas lover who decided to extend the celebrations to every day of the year, and so lived on turkey, trimmings and mince pies for 10 years, washed down with 400 litres of sherry.

There's method in his madness because he's a would-be pop star, and reckons a ditty about his bizarre behaviour could be turned into a hit record.

His ultimate goal is to get on to the Christmas edition of Top of the Pops, knocking Noddy Holder and the lads back out to Wolverhampton.

He's made a succession of stabs at a catchy tune and seasonal lyrics, but we were told by people who know about these things that he just keeps coming up with a turkey.

POOPER SCOOPER
Is irritable bowel syndrome a good topic for Christmas dinner conversation?

Philippa Davies had this and other vital party etiquette answers for Western Mail readers. She is their Mrs Motivator, "a top psychologist to Prime and Cabinet Ministers". Client confidentially denied us the names of the governmental figures who'd invested in her counselling. But her kitchen tip for troublesome interferers is: "Confuse them and flounce out," and we remember John Major applying this technique on more than one occasion.

Oh, and by the way, don't bring up your bowels.

BAD HOLIDAY
We saw an ad for a very cheap package holiday in Spain for the week before Christmas. Only snag was, the airport was down on the south coast, and we're in Scotland. But it seemed like a very pleasant change of scene, so we went for it. (We used your M6 book on the way down – which helped.)

It was six days, which meant we'd get back to the UK on Christmas Eve morning, and use that day to drive north again.

The holiday was fine. Reasonable weather and an escape from the pre-Christmas shopping syndrome, but when we returned to the Spanish airport for our flight back, we were told there might be some delay.

We hung round the sparse airport lounge for about four hours and were then invited to board our aircraft. We were all hot and irritable by now, and then we were told that there would be some further delays.

It was about an hour before the aircraft started up and moved away from the buildings. It taxied out towards a runway, but then it just sat on that spot for half an hour. Some passengers started to worry there was a technical problem and that the aircraft wasn't safe to fly. We couldn't get any sense out of the crew.

It was horribly hot in the aircraft and the air-conditioning didn't seem to be working.

We were then told that they were waiting for an engineer to check an instrument. Well, the engineer must have been in a different part of Spain, because nothing happened for another hour.

Some passengers were now demanding to get off, and several people had broken into their duty free and were swigging back alcohol, much against the wishes of the stewards, who said this wasn't permitted.

The heat levels continued to rise and became quite unbearable.

The airline's answer to this was to open a passenger door and position a big refrigeration unit on top of a hydraulic arm outside it, then put an electric fan to blow cold air from the giant fridge into the aircraft. It was pathetic.

One bloke - obviously the worse for drink - got up and stood right in front of the fan, cooling himself, and in the process denying other people the fragments of cooler air that this ridiculous system was providing.

He started dancing about at the edge of the open door, and then he decided to cross to the fridge itself, but he misjudged it and fell down the gap between the aircraft and the fridge.

The aircrew were very slow to respond. You got the feeling they felt he deserved to fall. They looked down to ground level and shouted at him.

A minute later we could see him limping away from the aircraft across the concourse towards the airport buildings.

Suddenly the crew closed the door, the fridge was pulled back, and the aircraft started up again.

We thought they were going to take us back to the buildings, but the plane headed out on to the runway.

The man who had jumped off was with three other blokes, all from Leeds, and none of them seemed terribly bothered that their mate was no longer with them.

The plane took off and got to England at lunchtime on Christmas Eve, where we were met by staff, who obviously didn't want to be around at that time and had reluctantly had to wait to receive us.

The six days in Spain just wasn't worth it. All we could think about over Christmas was that appalling morning stuck in the terrible aeroplane, and what happened to the idiot who fell off.

Sam Everest, Glasgow

LAST LAUGH

Two of the world's most popular comedians died on a Christmas Day: W.C. Fields in 1946 and Charlie Chaplin in 1977.

A funeral director told us that in her experience less people die on Christmas Day than on other days of the year. Her theory is that those departing don't want to be a nuisance to their relatives. It's not that they want to enjoy one more Christmas, and so hold on til Boxing Day.

GOING DOWN

I used to work for a fork lift truck firm in Manchester. I sometimes had to go up to Preston to do odd bits of work there. If there wasn't a van available, the accountants insisted you use a hire car for the journey.

The company with the car hire contract were based at a multi-storey car park.

On Christmas Eve morning I was asked to go to Preston to deal with a problem there. So I dashed down to the car hire office and was handed the keys for one of the vehicles that were kept on the fourth floor of the car park above.

I was assured that the car hire office would be manned until 5.30 that afternoon. I got to Preston and did what work I could, then, at about four, I started to drive back to base.

With my foot down, I managed to get back into Manchester just after five.

I drove straight up into the deserted multi-storey and parked the vehicle next to the other hire cars.

I hopped into the lift to head down to the offices. I pressed the button for the ground floor. The lift commenced its descent. Then it suddenly stopped and the lights went out.

I immediately realised someone (probably drunk) had turned the power off and was about to head off for their Christmas break.

I knew that I would not survive several days and nights in this small steel box so I screamed my head off and banged the sides of the lift as hard as I could. After about five minutes I heard a voice, and, half an hour later, the car park manager got me released.

All I could think about on Christmas Day was the fact I wasn't dead.

Peter Barnet, Middlesex

TRADES DESCRIPTIONS

There must be some law enabling us to claim a television licence refund or perhaps sue the BBC under the Consumer's Act.

Christmas programmes were absolutely diabolical.

Ken Hiles, Birmingham

BAD VIBES

My elder sister, Fanny, made our Christmas Day a truly terrible occasion because of her bizarre pursuit of Goth goals.

She'd become a Goth in the summer, and then in the autumn she turned her bedroom into a ghoulish grotty for Halloween.

She decided she liked the look of it so much she'd keep it like that.

When it got to Christmas she was scathing of traditional Christmas values and announced that it was essentially a pagan festival and that we would all regret not paying respects to the pagan Gods at this time of year instead of following the Christian traditions.

She didn't want to partake in any Christmas Day activities, but nevertheless she gave herself a Christmas present, which was a book of spells. Then, while Mum was doing the lunch, Fanny started doing spells in the living room, which included a curse on anyone who failed to recognise the pagan Gods.

Dad told her to shut up and stop being stupid, and an hour later he got chronic heartburn which Fanny told him was the curse.

Next Mum dropped her china gravy boat and broke it, which again Fanny attributed to the curse.

I now waited in anxiety for how the curse would affect me. Meanwhile Fanny went off to her room, and in the middle of the evening set her curtains on fire with a candle by mistake.

My Dad asked her if the pagan Gods had done this.

I worried for days about how the curse might hit me. Then it dawned on me that my sister, bless her, had been a curse on me that Christmas.

Frank Whittington, Lincoln

SOMETHING TO GET YOUR TEETH INTO

Over Christmas in Britain we get through 10 million turkeys, 25 million Christmas puddings, 35 million bottles of wine and 250 million pints of beer.

So averaged out to each adult, that means one person consumes a quarter of a turkey, half a pud, one bottle of wine and six pints of beer. Which doesn't sound so bad, does it.

Of course, for every person who's not having a beer at all, that means someone else has to drink 12 pints.

You can see how it can get out of hand quite quickly.

A TURKEY IS FOR LIFE

After all the horrible stories I had heard about turkeys being factory farmed in Thailand in the midst of dangers of avian flu that could spread to humans, I decided I would buy a local bird.

I went to a farm in Herefordshire and the farmer told me I could pick my very own turkey. I thought he meant from a variety of dressed birds in a freezer, but he meant from the barn in which they were living.

Now somewhat anxious, I went with him into the barn.

Not surprisingly, they all looked the same, and I started to think I was being ridiculous. But one caught my eye, and I pointed her out. The farmer moved through the birds to reach the one I'd picked. I was terrified he was going to wring its neck right there in front of me and the other turkeys, but he was finding its tag to identify it, and he made a note of its number and promised me that bird would be prepared for me during the next week.

I went home and felt terrible. I considered I'd personally condemned that turkey to death, and that if I hadn't have picked it out, it would continue to live a long and happy life alongside other members of its family.

For a couple of days I anguished over this dilemma, then I rang the farmer and confirmed that I wanted to buy the bird, but that I didn't want it killed.

I went and collected it in my car and brought it home and we kept it in the back garden for several days. Our neighbours thought it was very funny.

I became even more attached to the creature that I had now christened "Bootiful". Our garden wasn't a suitable place for Bootiful to reside, and so I tracked down a children's farm and handed her over to them, with assurances that she wouldn't end up on someone's plate.

You won't be surprised to know that I went vegetarian, and haven't looked back, though the rest of my family insisted on tucking into turkey (a frozen one from Tescos) on Christmas Day.

Pamela Hatten, Gloucester

I'VE BEEN TO BUTTERBALL

Where were you educated? Why 'Butterball University'.

So can say graduates of an intensive home economics course that is a prerequisite for call centre duties on America's Turkey Talk-line service.

During November and December forty five "ladies" dish out turkey preparation tips to 100,000 people at home who haven't a clue.

So, girls, enrol at Butterball, and then you can earn some seasonal pin money. It also gets you out of the house in the pre-Christmas period, though it's hardly going to take your mind off things.

SNEEZING AND STUFFING

Pointing out that that 20% of food poisoning outbreaks are poultry related, Powys Council Environmental Health team offered seasonal food safety advice to its citizens:

"Wash your hands after coughing, sneezing or touching pets. If you feel you must stuff the bird, make sure you take the stuffing weight into account."

THE PERFECT SOLUTION

There is no truth in the rumour that when some people saw the supermarket Product Recall notice in the papers on Saturday 11th December 2004, they immediately dashed out hoping to find an offending pack of Snowman iced jam tarts.

Why would they?

Because the firm had announced that some of the snowman plaques still had plastic backing attached to them and so could present a choking hazard.

What sane person could see this as an opportunity to get rid of Grannie and then sue a supermarket group for the tragic loss and distress suffered on Christmas Day?

Perish the thought.

BEWARE OF THE BOWL

Kitchens are full of dangerous things – knives, food mixers, and… gravy.

Yes, according to the Royal Society for the Prevention of Accidents, a significant number of people were injured by exploding gravy in the microwave oven on Christmas Day.

Apparently they don't follow the instructions properly, the stuff suddenly burst out of the bowl and the cook opens the door in a hurry and gets scalded.

TAKEAWAY

Those of us lucky to live within ten miles of Cardiff need never worry again about the anguish of preparing a Christmas meal.

We can order a takeaway instead. No, not a run-of-the-mill pizza, curry or Chinese. We're talking turkey - with stuffing, sprouts, and roast potatoes.

Ring-a-Roast tills rang out with joy as south Welsh Mums invested in this instant solution to the challenges of Christmas catering.

The red and white chiller van proved a welcome sight in the valleys. *"Far more useful than some stupid Santa,"* one kitchen-phobic mother admitted.

The service was the brainchild of Alun Morgan (who told us he can't rub two eggs together). It was his mother-in-law's talent for turkey and trimmings that inspired him to investigate the possibilities of providing her delicious dish to all and sundry.

His family were the guinea pigs for the trials. Once they'd got the formula right they advertised the proposition and got plenty of takers – even from people on boats in Cardiff Bay – and it wasn't yet Christmas.

Alun wonders if the concept could be franchised. Mouth-watering mother-in-law meals-on-wheels?

Maybe.

PIG IN

My brother David had been on his own for four years since his marriage broke up, so we were pleased when he told us he'd met someone new.

We thought the decent thing was to invite David and his new girlfriend to come and stay with us over Christmas.

They turned up on Christmas Eve about 7 o'clock, having driven from London. We hadn't met "Fiona" before, and hoped that we'd all get on.

I know one shouldn't jump to opinions about strangers, but the first thing I was aware about her was her weight. She seemed enormous. My brother's not slim - none of us are - but this woman was just in a different league altogether. She seemed friendly enough, but couldn't wait to get in the kitchen. I'd prepared some supper, but she insisted on having a handful of biscuits while she was being introduced to everyone. And she emptied the bowls of nuts and crisps I'd left in the living room.

We sat down for supper and she scoffed her way through whatever she could get her hands on.

And they told us they'd had a snack at a motorway service area on the way.

I decided my brother was mad to have got involved with this monster. He just smiled a lot, as if her behaviour was mildly amusing, and nothing to worry about.

In the night I couldn't sleep for wondering if we had enough food in the house, and also how we could get rid of both of them as quickly as possible.

My husband tried to put my mind at rest by pointing out there were several loaves of bread in the freezer and we could just give her a couple of these to make a giant sandwich with.

On Christmas morning she had what I would describe as breakfast for two, and then she offered to help me in the kitchen. Frankly I was worried she'd eat all the Christmas meal in a semi-raw state.

She then confided in me that she was planning on going on a diet in the New Year. I felt like saying: Why don't you start right now?

She kept suggesting I do more bacon, more sausages, more vegetables, more everything. I pointed out the food was to last us for three days.

She seemed alarmed at this prospect. It was like she was addicted to food.

We eventually sat down to our Christmas meal and, as we'd all expected, she got stuck into everything with a determination bordering on the manic.

My husband gave her a second helping of turkey before the rest of us had finished our first, and within a couple of minutes she'd gorged that and was then helping herself to some more meat - which was when my husband blew up at her.

He yelled at her and told her that her behaviour was completely unacceptable and that she was a rude pig who needed medical help – physical and mental. David just sat there with a silly smile on his face.

She told David she wanted to go home, so David got up and they packed their bags and left straightaway.

We were just immensely relieved, but I was of course worried for my brother. He rang us on Boxing Day to say they had split up and he was eternally grateful to my husband for having confronted her appalling greed.

Apparently they had stopped at two service areas on the way down the M4 and she had had snacks at both.

Patty Freemantle, Somerset

80

DINNER IN BITS

Our electric oven died on Christmas morning, so I was forced to try to cook our meal in our very small microwave, for which I'd lost the instruction booklet. It wasn't easy.

For a start the turkey wouldn't fit inside, so my partner had to hack it into four chunks using his tenon saw.

But one quarter wasn't enough for the six of us who were going to eat together, so I had to do two quarters, one after the other.

Then I tried microwaving portions of vegetables, but some got burnt and the others turned soggy.

We ended up simply having shrivelled turkey sandwiches with a raw carrot salad.

Penny Faraday, Market Harborough

RIDE IT OUT

The Christmas I'll never forget was when I was about seven, and we were invited to my uncle's crumbling pile outside Malmesbury. Uncle Dennis was a rather grand old fellow who lived on his own and had a great love of horses, hunting and other country pursuits.

He'd got a woman in to do the Christmas lunch. She stayed in the kitchen whilst Uncle plied us with drink. He was all for me and my sister having mulled wine, but my parents resisted. Eventually the meal was served up. It wasn't a turkey but red meat that I found sour and stringy, but I was starving so got on with it.

Uncle kept going on about what a special day this was and what a treat we were having.

My mother said she wasn't hungry, and didn't touch her food.

At the end of the meal, Uncle proposed a toast: "To Sadie" (his horse).

Dad said: "Where is she?" And Uncle Dennis replied: "Inside you."

Yes, he'd served up his dead horse for our Christmas lunch.

My big sister immediately ran outside and threw up.

Mum said she realised what it was straightaway, and Dad tried to make out it was all fine and that a horse was essentially nothing more than a streamlined cow.

My uncle now burst into tears and cried inconsolably for five minutes.

We left the house shortly afterwards and never went back until his funeral.

David Jolley, Bristol

TURKEY TIKKA

My 17-year old brother, Mark, said turkey was "so yesterday" and demanded a curry for his Christmas lunch.

My mother refused to indulge him and prepared a lovely meal as usual. As she started to serve it up, my brother produced a catering can of curry sauce, opened it with a tin opener and poured some of it cold over his food.

Mum was furious.

Mark ate it all and said it was delicious.

At our next meal he did the same thing again.

After that Mum boiled up the sauce in a pan and kept it on the stove. Mark had some of the hot curry sauce on every dish until it and the turkey were finished. I don't think he enjoyed it, but you had to admire his determination.

Melanie Fellows, Darlington

BONJOUR

My uncle married a Frenchwoman, and they came and stayed with my parents one Christmas.

On Christmas Day Andree seemed immensely appreciative of all the festivities that my mother laid on.

Then on Boxing Day she said she would give us a taste of her typical family Christmas.

She'd brought lots of ingredients for a complicated fish dish, and she now set to work with a vengeance.

Andree swore a lot in French as preparations continued, and the house stank of rotting fish all morning.

By lunchtime we were all dreading what might be served up.

And our fears were well-founded, because she dished out this dreadful soup with fish guts and eyes, and raw shell-fish floating round in it. It was like a bucket of sludge from the Marseilles docks.

For my uncle's sake, we all forced down a few spoonfuls of this disgusting fare. After they'd gone, my Dad told us he thought Andree was getting us back for the Battle of Trafalgar.

Paul Findleyson, Maidstone

CHEESY

God moves in mysterious ways, perhaps few more difficult to digest than providing mankind with an image of the Virgin Mary on a slice of toast.

Run-of-the-mill cold cheese slid under the grill. What came out a few minutes later was a fuzzy impression of the Madonna, according to the inspired cook. You may mock, but the cheese on toast was preserved for posterity and subsequently sold on e-bay for $20,000.

Study those Brussels sprouts. One might double as Elvis Presley's bollocks.

THRUPPENCE FOR YOUR THOUGHTS

Mum was always busy working right up to Christmas Eve and it always seemed to take her by surprise. Christmas preparations consisted of a mad dash round the shops on Christmas Eve to buy sprouts and Christmas pudding and, normally, a chicken. One year she only remembered the bird at half four when we were in the middle of hanging up pink and green crepe paper chains in the dining room, and she had a mighty panic. Grandma and a few odd aunts were coming for Christmas dinner, which made it worse.

Mum flew out of the house in a whirlwind with Dad in tow. He was to drive her round the shops to see if there were any chickens left. There were no frozen birds on polystyrene pallets readily available in those days; no supermarkets that stay open till late and never run out of things. Only the empty butcher's shop, empty of chickens, that is. Plenty of sausages, but you couldn't have just sausages at Christmas, especially not with grandmother and the aunts coming. Dad's car returned with Mum waving a paper bag jubilantly. "I found a cooked chicken at the delicatessen," she triumphed. "So I don't even have to cook the darn thing!"

I remember the aggravation. Mum was locked in a steaming kitchen for what seemed hours doing battle with the sprouts, parsnips and roast potatoes, trying to make sure that everything got cooked at the right time and the sprouts didn't go soggy or the chicken dry up. And the Christmas pudding was steaming away in a colander over a saucepan of boiling water all morning. No microwaves then. (Mind you, how would they have coped with the silver three-

penny pieces stuffed in the pudding?) And the rest of the family sat around sipping thimbles of ginger wine and saying "That smells good" every half hour or so.

Grandma looked disparagingly at the dark shrivelled bird, and said in her most withering voice, "That's a pre-cooked chicken!"

Oh the disgrace of it!!! No amount of Sauterne (Dad's once-a-year wine) could wash it away. Mum would never live it down.

Grandma and the aunts munched balefully, their teeth clattering in disapproval with every mouthful. Plates were cleared, crackers pulled and paper hats donned in a travesty of Christmas cheer and then the Pudding was served. Mum poured a small amount of cream sherry over it and tried to ignite it with no success. The sprig of holly was removed and large portions doled out to the assembled wrinklies who fell upon it voraciously.

Grandma suddenly started choking and going purple in the face, all her chins wobbling frantically. There was instant concern, turning to panic as she went from bad to worse.

Suddenly Dad loomed up behind her and administered a hefty thump to her back between the shoulder blades, which were in there somewhere. She was visibly shocked but still choking, so he thumped her again, with some relish, I observed.

Suddenly a threepenny bit flew out of her mouth and landed in the custard bowl. A gasping and slobbering Grandma then collapsed melodramatically and demanded to be taken upstairs to lie down, where – mercifully - she stayed for the rest of the afternoon.

Eileen Burzynska, Essex

STUFF IT

I bought my girlfriend a black PVC corset with metal studs on. Yes, I know it was more a present for me rather than her.

When she opened it under the Christmas tree, she gave me a half smile, which I took to be a good sign. However she was understandably preoccupied by the fact that my parents were coming round for Christmas dinner which she was about to cook.

I thought everything was going fine, until she invited us all into the dining room and there was the corset wrapped round the turkey.

She'd even gone to the trouble of putting some black stockings on the bird's legs. My Dad could see the funny side, but my mother sulked all afternoon.

And I had backache from wincing.

Chris Gibbens, Nottingham

"Fancy two weeks in Turkey?"

KIDS' STUFF

CURSE OF THE NURSERY

I thought I was going to miss our office Christmas party because our first baby was born in the first week of December, and my wife needed every second of help with his early weeks.

I was resigned to not attending the event and came home from work at the usual time to take over from Mum.

But my wife - bless her - wanted me to join in the fun and suggested I go along for a couple of hours at least.

I did the usual chores and put little James to bed, then got changed ready to nip out for a while.

Just as I was opening the front door, James started crying, so I went back upstairs to attend to him.

I walked him round his nursery for ten minutes patting him on the back.

He calmed down and I put him back in his cot and he went to sleep.

My wife was now asleep in the living room, so I left her a note and nipped off.

I got to the pub where my workmates were, and they were all fairly sloshed by now.

I just felt I shouldn't be there, so once I'd briefly shown my face to my boss, I turned round and went home.

When I got in, my wife gave me a very strange look. She was shocked to see that I'd come into the house with vomit splashed down the back of my jacket. She was horrified at the behaviour of the drunken idiots I worked with.

I took my jacket off and realised our baby had been sick down my back before I'd gone out for my very brief night on the town.

Simon Parson, Braintree

BAD JUDGE

You're a Dad living apart from your wife, and sharing the parental functions for your five year old son.

You and his Mum cannot agree to the arrangements for Christmas.

You think he should spend the time with you. Mum doesn't want that.

No solution except to go to court and seek expert advice.

You will explain to your lawyer the issues of your case. How having Christmas at your home is in the best interests of the child.

You practice your arguments, refine your speech.

There's tension in the air as you enter the Italian courtroom.

The judge is in a hurry. And he's in a bad mood.

Does he want to hear how you have done so much so far for your son and have excellent plans for his welfare and edification over the Christmas holidays?

Nope. He tosses a coin and, on the basis of that, announces Mum's won the case.

CAUGHT IN

At the age of five I couldn't sleep on Christmas Eve and so got up and went to the door of my parents' bedroom. I could see Santa in bed with my Mum, so I went back to my bed.

I didn't tell anyone about this for years. But every Christmas Eve I would have a word with my Dad, asking him if he was going to stay in the house and keep an eye on Mum. I must have been about eleven before it dawned on me that what I'd seen originally had been my Dad dressed up as Santa in bed with Mum. I never told my parents.

Lorna Perkins, Marlborough

TAKE THAT BACK

When I was about seven I got a real surprise as a Christmas present. It was a great big box, and when I unwrapped it I was delighted to discover it contained a metal detector. This wasn't something I'd asked for, or had even though would make a good gift. But I was immediately fascinated by its prospects.

However my Mum took it off me straightaway and went out into the back garden and started using it. She said she was testing it. She kept swinging it over a flower bed. After a couple of minutes she got a bleep on the headphones. She stuck her fingers into the soil and pulled out her wedding ring which she'd lost a few days earlier.

I thought she'd done this as a trick to demonstrate how good the thing was, but it turned out she had really lost the ring and really did find it thanks to the metal detector.

But she now told me the machine was no good and so would have to go back. She put it back in the box and wouldn't let me touch it. I spent all Boxing Day digging in the back garden with a small spade.

She took the metal detector back to Argos and got her money back.

That whole next year I begged her to buy me one.

Next Christmas there was a second hand one wrapped up for me under the tree, but it wasn't the same and it didn't seem to work properly.

Ben Hammonds, Uxbridge

DIFFERENT WORLD

I don't want to sound like a Scrooge, but there's something really seriously wrong in the world when millions of children in Africa are dying in childhood from disease and poverty and meanwhile, since Christmas, our estate is plagued by fat louts menacing pedestrians by riding round on electrically powered scooters that cost hundreds of pounds.

These youngsters need exercise, not indulgence.

Martin Willow, Kent

TERRIBLE TEDDY

It's a bottle shaped like a teddy. And what's inside? A brightly-coloured drink. Aw, what a nice pressie for the little ones.

But wait. Let Staffordshire Consumer Services Department undertake a forensic test on the contents of the liquid.

Two conclusions: It tastes horrible. And it's contaminated with considerable amounts of bacteria.

Em, right, so that car boot bargain ain't such a good idea after all.

A BARBIE SULK

My little sister, Chloe, worked herself up into a frenzy about having a Barbie bicycle for Christmas, and so was beside herself when Father Christmas and my parents failed to bring her one.

She stormed off to her room and wouldn't come out til Boxing Day.

Mum tried to talk sense into her from the landing. Mum said: "I bet Barbie wouldn't sulk like that", to which Chloe yelled back: "I bet she bloody would!"

Phil Patching, Sheffield

DON'T BUY DODGY DVDS

"The lady's got no pants on" was the remark which alerted us to the fact that the cartoon DVD our children had been given by a neighbour included something other than what it said on the box.

Melissa Grundy, Grantham

BURNT OUT

When I was seven I went to my Dad's flat for Christmas. On the morning my Mam came to see me and give me my present. It was a big American model car but it needed a battery and there wasn't one in the box. So my Dad went off to the corner shop to get a battery.

As soon as he'd gone, Mam took his half cooked turkey out of his oven and put all his clothes inside instead, then poured his brandy over them and lit them. Then she took me and the turkey off to her flat about three streets away.

Dad came round and banged on the door of Mam's flat about three times that day, but Mam wouldn't open the door. One of the neighbours called the police who came round and took him away.

He spent Christmas night in the police station.

He left the toy car on the landing, but there was no battery with it.

I was really cross with him for not having got a battery. None of the rest of it mattered to me until years later.

David, Powys

JUST A BIT OF FUN

My cousin Jonathan was a wild child. I was a couple of years older than him but he terrified me with his anarchic behaviour. He got a Tonka truck for Christmas and on Boxing Day he had it out in our back garden. He managed to get into my parents' shed and he found a can of paraffin, which he poured into the open back of the truck. I was sure this wasn't a good thing to do, but didn't have the bottle to stop him, or to tell the adults inside what was going on. He got a lighter and lit the paraffin in the truck and started to kick it along.

He set fire to his jeans and the truck rolled into the side of the shed, tipping burning paraffin along the wooden base. We managed to put out his jeans before his leg got burnt, but we couldn't stop the flames spreading up the side of the shed which created a big fire and a Boxing Day call out for the fire brigade.

Matthew Parnell, Evesham

ONLY PLAYING

Discount shops in the north of England last year were selling small hand-held electronic games that took the biscuit for bad taste: 'Laden versus USA' featured a liquid crystal display showing Osama Bin Laden flying an aircraft towards New York skyscrapers.

The toy came from China – which is where 95% of the world's toys are manufactured.

THE LONG TERM

I'll never forget the Christmas when I suffered attempts at revenge by one of my school pupils who bore me a grudge after I stopped him from going on the school trip because of bad behaviour.

He hung around outside my house almost every day of the holiday, sitting on the wall across the road, looking daggers in my direction.

I blame that Saturday morning TV programme Tiswas for establishing a culture of disrespect for teachers. They used to throw green gunk over teachers in a cage and everyone was supposed to find this hilarious.

Well, no wonder discipline in the classroom deteriorated, when the person who should have been given respect was treated as a figure of fun. And that culture is now instilled in the parents whose offspring are now attending school with a terrible dismissive attitude to the people in charge and trying to keep order.

Connie Bellamy, Dublin

BEST WISHES

As an end-of-term activity in our school we got the Year Two children to write letters to Father Christmas. One seven year old wrote: "I would like a bike and the Harry Potter game and a gun to shoot Nathan Mills."

Naturally we had to bring these aspirations to the attention of the relevant parents.

Hilary Spender, Golders Green

BOX OF TRICKS

When I was young Chemistry Sets were popular Christmas presents for boys. My friends and I all asked Santa for one, and most of us had our wishes met. The boxes were full of things that these days would probably fail any Health and Safety test. But if you followed the instructions you could undertake a series of innocuous experiments.

However we were soon drawn to more dramatic possibilities and so raided kitchen cupboards and the cellar for more exciting ingredients.

A couple of us poured a concoction of chemicals into a saucepan and started to heat it on the stove. The cocktail suddenly burst up and out in front of us.

The bubbling, smelly goo made a hole in mother's linoleum (that's floor covering, for younger readers) and fifty years later, I still have scars on my ear, neck and arm.

George Callam, Hackney

PLASTIC PLEASE

I know lots of people scoff at synthetic Christmas trees, but we have had one for the last five years since we discovered our daughter, Melissa, is allergic to the real thing.

Her first Christmas saw her break out in eczema, but because she had eaten so many different things we couldn't track down what was causing the problem. We took her to the doctor for tests to try to identify the culprit.

However the eczema cleared up in the second week of January, so we didn't proceed with any medication.

Only 11 months later when my husband brought home another freshly cut tree, and a day later Melissa had patches of eczema on her arms and legs, did we realise that the tree was the cause.

We give her some steroids over the Christmas period so she can get through school and parties without suffering from this very unseasonal syndrome.

Alice Hopton, Manchester

GOSPEL

What inspired cartoon producer Steve Legg to invest considerable time and money into creating an animated film about the birth of Christ?

He overhead a child say: *"Why was Jesus named after a swear word?"*

87

DOUBLE LIFE

My husband and I are separated. William, our four year old, pestered us to buy him a big electronic robot toy for Christmas. Both of us told him it cost too much, but without telling the other, we both caved in and so he got one from Father Christmas at my house on Christmas morning, then another from his Dad at his flat in the afternoon.

William didn't tell his father he'd had the same toy that morning. He kept each robot at the relevant address for a couple of weeks, then took the one here to his Dad's so they could fight each other.

Susan Blakedow, Ealing

"I won't be needing a Playstation as stated in my letter. I've found one behind my Mum's wardrobe."

ONE TO REMEMBER

3 out of 10 people go overdrawn for Christmas.
One in four of us avoid Christmas kissing.
One in 100 Brits buy no Christmas gifts.

ON THE UP

I came back to England the day before Christmas Eve to spend the holiday with my family and friends. I got the Eurostar to Waterloo, then took the underground to reach Paddington.

I was halfway up the escalator at Paddington when up ahead of me I saw an elderly lady stumble at the point where the escalator levels out. She dropped her shopping bags and they started to fall towards me. I was going to try to grab them when I realised she was starting to fall as well.

I left go of my luggage and ran up the steps just as she started to tumble backwards down the up escalator. I managed to get hold of her firmly and stop her falling. I gripped her and we both travelled upwards and I heaved her off the end of the escalator.

We collapsed in a heap just by the end of the system, which no-one had seen fit to stop.

People came to our aid, and her shopping and my luggage were gathered up from somewhere below and brought back to us.

Station staff turned up and helped the lady away in a wheelchair, and I went home to relate my story about the good fortune that had caused me to reach that point on the escalator at the very moment that woman was in need.

I told my pal Phil about this in the pub the next day and at the end of my tale of good samaritanism, all he had to say was: "What colour knickers did she have on?"

Stewart Goodall, Perigueux

COCK UP

A popular TV prankster was going to have the tables turned on him for the series's Christmas special.

The programme producers secretly decided to set up tiny hidden cameras in the fellow's flat, and catch him at home unexpectedly, as he had done to dozens of others.

Whilst our hero was at a football match, his girlfriend let the technicians into the apartment. The boys set up their gear and retired to their van parked round the back of the block.

Mr Clever Dick comes back home and his gorgeous girlfriend makes an excuse to pop out for a pint of milk, leaving the star of the show alone in his living room.

She sneaks into the disguised outside broadcast van for last minute instructions from the crew and, blow me, on some of the TV screens behind the control panel, she was shocked to see Prince Prankster doing something disgusting.

Clue? She'd seen him picking his nose plenty of times.

IT WOOD HAPPEN TO US

Our friends invited us to spend Christmas with them in an unusual setting – an old timber mill outside a delightful village in a big forest.

We were sure this would give a feel for a natural Christmas, away from commerce, and amidst wonderful examples of the work of Mother Nature.

The mill had been converted to a holiday home and we would be the first people to use it.

We arrived on Christmas Eve afternoon, loaded up with everything we might need over the holidays. The building was very utilitarian, but in a magical setting.

The ladies started to prepare a meal in the kitchen whilst the men collected firewood – not difficult in this setting - and lit the big stove in the middle of the main room.

Perhaps we over-loaded the stove, or maybe it had been re-assembled incorrectly after servicing, but after half an hour it was crackling in an alarming way. We started to try to cool it down, by removing some of the logs from inside. Foolishly, one of the ladies poured some cold water over it and this caused the cast iron to crack. Suddenly there was burning timber spilling out on to the wooden floor. You would have thought four adults could have brought control to the emergency but it got out of hand very swiftly and we only had one bucket and one fire extinguisher.

We were amazed as well as dismayed to see the whole of the room being so quickly overtaken with flames.

To cut a long story short, the whole complex burnt down and the spruces around the buildings caught on fire.

We escaped with our cars and our lives, but an area of woodland was destroyed before firefighters – who had to come from a great distance - managed to isolate the fire.

Josef Gruber, Oberndorf

GRATE TIME

We moved to our newly-converted barn in the summer, which gave us time to furnish the main rooms through the autumn. The reception rooms were large and so required new carpet which came in October; then in November I had time to organise our existing furniture with a mind to making our living room inhabitable for guests by Christmas.

By December I had got the house fairly well organised, and my husband and I then prepared the living room for a Christmas Eve party. We put up decorations, and the whole place looked very civilised.

One thing we had yet to try was the fire in the living room.

We bought an iron grate, and late afternoon on Christmas Eve, a couple of hours before our guests were due to arrive, my husband lit the fire in the traditional way – some rolled up newspaper, a few sticks and heaps of coal.

It was the icing on the cake and gave the room a beautiful seasonal quality.

We were both in the kitchen, focused on last minute preparations when a huge explosion came from the living room. We ran in to discover the fire had blown out of the hearth and was scattered across the room. Burning coals were lying on the new carpet, and had even reached my sofa. We used a tray and a plate to scoop the burning coal up and back into the hearth and threw wet towels over the smouldering patches on the carpet and sofa.

It turned out the builder had used a big slab of slate for the base of the fireplace and when this had become very hot, it had split apart, hurling the heavy metal grate out of its place.

Gilian Wrexham, Kidderminster

KILLER SNOW

An extremely heavy snowstorm brought parts of Cleveland, Ohio, to a complete halt on Christmas Eve 2004.

The weight of ice on trees broke branches, which fell across power lines, knocking out all electricity over huge areas.

This affected an airline computer system, that meant 1,100 flights were cancelled, and 30,000 passengers were left stranded in various airport lounges, unable to reach their Christmas destinations.

And seven motorists in the state died of heart attacks that day whilst trying to shovel snow.

VOW NEVER AGAIN

Christmas week in Albufiera - and an escape from the English winter, and demanding marriage counselling work. We could look forward to long days of sun, sand and secular pleasures.

Okay, so the resort was a bit on the quiet side, our hotel less than average, and we could only find one decent restaurant - run by a young English couple, Martin and Clare, who didn't overcook the veg and did a nice line in moules marinieres. We went there every evening, but gradually realised that for Martin and Clare all was not well on the marriage front.

We'd hear snatches of arguments floating out of the kitchen: "...working my fingers to the bone...you're always out playing golf ... mother was right ... never wanted to come here in the first place ... sick of sodding sardines ..."

As we sat waiting for our meal on our third visit, I whispered to Julia "I could try a bit of counselling."

"We're supposed to be on holiday," she hissed. "Stay out of it."

Christmas Day came, and so did lashing wind and rain. But at least we knew we had a table booked at Martin and Clare's for their Christmas special.

We got there at eight, but found the place all locked up. A bedraggled note on the door said 'Closed due to unforeseen circumstances. Sorry'.

The only other place open was the 'Bengal Star'. We and the waiters glared at our un-Christmassy curry.

Julia said darkly, "Don't ever bring me to Portugal again."

Then added, "And when we get home, I think we need to talk ..."

John Elkington, Worcestershire

WHO YOU GONNA CALL?

Samaritans get less calls on Christmas Day than typical December days, but year on year the number for the month is rising by around 20% per annum.

136,064 despairing calls were made to the helpline during December 2004, of which 3,547 were on Christmas Day.

SPLASH OUT

You know those stupid charity swims in the North Sea that mad people undertake on Christmas Day for 10 seconds of exposure on the telly. And there's always one old bloke who looks like he'd be better off tucked up in bed with a hot water bottle.

Well, everyone's worse fears came to pass on Christmas Day last year when an old geezer staggered out of the sea after a quick freezing dip and died on the beach in front of hundreds of people like me who wanted to see something unusual on Christmas morning.

Paddy Filton, Great Yarmouth

TEXAN CRAWL

If you live in Texas, you're all tooled up to drive your gas guzzler round with the air conditioning on, keeping you cool every day of the year.

So why should Christmas Day be any different?

Well, it was a white one. Yes, a Texan snowstorm – which is not something anyone under the age of 80 could remember before.

And Texan motorists didn't know quite what to do.

They couldn't get their heads round the fact that there was slippery stuff on the roads.

So they just roared along in their usual manner – and were then surprised when they kept skidding into other vehicles.

Stepping out to inspect the damage, they discovered it was colder out of the 4x4 than in.

Ooh, strange.

And their leader's telling them climate change ain't true.

WET BLANKETS

Our family went to my mother-in-law's for Christmas. We set off on Christmas morning in reasonable weather, but by the time we had travelled the 40 miles into Cheshire, snow had started to fall. Over the next couple of days it got colder and colder. When we headed back to Manchester it was absolutely freezing. We reached our house – a semi in the suburbs – and as we pulled up I noticed the front window curtains were looking odd. They seemed dark and stained.

My husband opened the front door and saw that the carpet was soaked, and we could hear water running.

A pipe had burst next to the cold water tank in the attic. The whole of the house was soaked. Downstairs was like a shallow pool, and the wallpaper was peeling off most of the walls. In the living room there was a complete mess under a big hole in the ceiling. The water had gathered in our bedroom above and had dropped through the floor, along with most of the plaster.

We turned off the water at the stop tap.

The lights were fused and we didn't dare turn the electric back on for fear of causing the whole wet house to become live.

Our children were in tears, and I wasn't far off.

It was a nightmare.

We returned to my mother-in-law's in the afternoon and stayed there for three months until the house was slowly brought back to normal.

Ann Allport, Manchester

DRIVING YOU MAD

Christmas is for the kids. That's what they say. So you do your best.

Some presents. Lots to eat and drink. And, okay then, your niece is only twelve, but you let her have a little alcohol – after all, it's Christmas.

So she later helps herself to a bit more. Then she helps herself to your car keys, and next minute she's driving round Swindon in your motor.

The family called the police, who tracked her down and discovered she was at nearly double the legal alcohol limit.

And so a suburban teenager suddenly became famous.

Yes, it's official. She's now Britain's youngest drunk driver.

ACTS OF GOD?

There's probably no reason to believe that more mass tragedies take place around Christmas than at other times of the year, but perhaps there's a greater sense of poignancy about the loss of loved ones during the season of goodwill, when we aim to spend quality time with our families.

Last year's Boxing Day tsunami was one of the biggest disasters in living memory, but the newspapers are never short of a horrific headline in the season of happy wishes.

To help us think ourselves lucky, here are a few, randomly picked, about random victims:

A fire in New York a week before Christmas 1835 got seriously out of control because the hydrants were frozen so the fire officers couldn't get water on to the flames. They eventually had to dynamite buildings to create a fireproof gap which the flames could not cross.

December 28th 1908 an earthquake shook Sicily and claimed 70,000 lives.

A week before Christmas 1917 a troop train in the Alps derailed killing 500 soldiers. Wartime censorship meant this was kept secret for two years.

The following year, a week before Christmas a Chinese earthquake in Kansu killed 180,000.

Twelve years later on Christmas Day the same Chinese province suffered another quake that killed 70,000.

Snow fell to a depth of more than half a metre on Boxing Day 1947 in New York. 77 people died from the resulting cold or accidents.

On Christmas Eve 1953 the bridge carrying a train crossing a swollen river in New Zealand collapsed, plunging hundreds into freezing cold water, many of whom were never recovered.

A few days before Christmas in 1961 a Brazilian circus worker with a grievance set fire to the circus tent in the middle of a performance, killing 300. Em, yes, this last act wasn't an Act of God. It was a circus act.

SECOND COMING

Back in the Seventies I was a committed hippy. I spent a couple of years meandering around the Mediterranean, mindlessly bumming my way from one beach to another. In the second year I spent quite a lot of time in north Africa, hitching between settlements on the northern side of the Sahara. Occasionally this meant you had to walk for a day or two, which at first I found scary, but then got used to. I had long, straggly blond hair and a long beard and wore a white djellaba.

A lorry once dropped me off at a point near the Algerian border which left me with quite a trek to the nearest village, which was well off the beaten track.

Loaded up with water and oranges, I made my way towards this oasis. I could see a bunch of small pink buildings ahead surrounded by palm trees. It sat in a valley and I was at the top of a ridge half a mile away.

As I walked towards the place children spotted me and came out to greet me. They were affectionate and respectful. Then some of their parents started to approach me. They too treated me with great honour. I was received into the little community like a disciple. My local language skills were very poor, so there was a lot of pointing and gesturing, and it seemed almost as if they saw me as some sort of saviour or saint who had come to meet them and therefore bring good fortune on them.

Part of me was delighted at this sense of privilege, part of me found it a bit freaky. But, so as to not hurt their feelings, I went along with things and kissed their children and put my hands on and prayed for their sickly elderly relatives. They washed me and fed me and gave me a good bed for the night.

I couldn't stick more of their adoration, so in the morning, I made my excuses and left, and headed back for the road in the hope of another lorry lift.

Ten years later I was in the north of England working as a sound recordist on a low budget film. The movie was taking a break for Christmas, and I was going back to southern California. My flight was from Heathrow and so I decided to hitch down the M1 (old habits die hard).

A businessman picked me up and we headed south. Over the journey of several hours we got to talking about all sorts of things. He was a very focused guy, running his own stationery firm, with a family in Reading, and involved in a lot of Christian charity work, which he was going to spend several days on prior to Christmas.

He explained that he had been a drop-out when he was younger and had hung around Morocco and Algeria dealing in drugs for a number of years.

Then he had a life changing experience. He'd been thrown out of a jeep near an Algerian border crossing after an argument over hashish. He'd found his way to a village and the people there had looked after him with great kindness for several days. They told him that the Prophet had visited their village and that this great honour had brought good fortune on the people, which they now shared with strangers.

I asked the businessman to describe the location of the village and what it looked like.

I was sure this was where I had been and that I was the person that those villagers had perceived of as a Prophet.

The Christian businessman was kind enough to take me all the way to Heathrow. As we headed for the airport, I wondered if I should tell him my story of having visited that village ten years previously.

I didn't.

I wonder if he'll read this.

George Coen, Santa Monica

"I just had the most wonderful dream! — I dreamt Christmas was over!"

NO SIGN OF DICK

We must feel for the Daily Mail's theatre critic Quentin Letts. He has to sit through so many shows around the country each year, whether he wants to or not. Yes, okay, he does get paid.

However with that burden of theatrical endeavour upon his shoulders, you might think his attendance at his daughter's school Nativity Play would be nothing other than a busman's holiday.

Far from it.

His review was characteristically colourful and textured, containing some distinctly philosophical observations on the nature of drama and how seasonal endeavours in school halls can so easily eclipse the proscenium arched posturings of professional actors.

He was full of praise for the teachers who organise the little ones to gather round the manger and mug up on their dialogue.

One smart teacher was foresighted enough to give Quentin's six year old daughter, Eveleen, a lead role – Mary, no less. (Of course, how many junior school drama teachers can look forward to reviews for their efforts in national newspapers?).

Miss Letts's performance was not absolutely perfect. She dropped the baby Jesus, but quickly picked up the plastic doll and tucked it back in its swaddling clothes - all of which delighted Dad, clearly generating considerably more joy in his heart than much of what had passed through the West End in the previous twelve months.

LARGE MISTAKE

I'll never forget taking my children to Dick Whittington one year. Top of the bill were Little and Large, who at that time had had years of popular Saturday night entertainment programmes under their belts.

My six and seven year olds were delighted at the prospect of seeing real TV stars live on stage.

Most of the pantomime was standard fare, and I was happy to sit through it, but in the Second Act the two stars invited kids out of the audience to come up and join in a song.

Little was very personable and good at encouraging children to feel at ease on the stage, but the fat one, Large, seemed to have a manic quality that I think some children found quite menacing.

My daughter, Juliette, put up her hand to go on stage, and Little picked her out. She got a chance of singing a few bars of some stupid song on a big screen, but I was horrified when Large produced a toilet roll and started to make distasteful jokes at my innocent daughter's expense.

Marian Foxton, Bracknell

LET'S PUT ON A SHOW

How do you get started in pantomime?

1. Get hold of a script

2. Persuade people to take part.

Here's a short sample to help you capture the hearts and minds of potential participants:

'Aladdin' by Derek Dwyer and Merlin Price. Scene 5:

"Widow Twanky's cottage. As curtain opens, the Dame is seen to be doing an

impersonation of Julie Andrews.

DAME: (sings) "The house is alive, with the piles of washing! The socks, vests and knickers, from a thousand homes!" An' I wish they'd stayed there. Oooh, I hate washing! Don't you just hate washing (Repartee with audience)

I tell you, working in a laundry is no job for someone with a delicate sense of smell (sniffs armpits). Oooooooh!"

There you go. Bit more along the same lines and you're in business.

(This whole script and more at www.pantoscripts.com)

HE'S NOT BEHIND YOU

I've always been happy to help out behind the scenes with our amateur dramatics company endeavours, but I'm not one for going on stage.

But one year the regulars mounted an elaborate production of Sinbad.

They couldn't rustle up an Ebenezer (who was a villain with magical powers in our version of the script), so I was persuaded to take on this small role.

Unfortunately my scenes required sudden black-outs for dramatic effect, when I would appear or disappear from the middle of the stage.

Despite my nerves, the first night went reasonably well, but on the second evening of the show I became distracted at one point and, at the moment when all the lights went out for me to make a quick exit, I lost my bearings and walked in the wrong direction. Instead of sliding into the wings I stepped off the front of the stage and fell down on to the floor of the church hall. When the lights came back on, back stage staff were mystified. I had completely disappeared. Only the front row of the audience knew where I was. Lying in front of them, somewhat bruised and extremely embarrassed. I had to get up and walk out the emergency exit to get back behind the scenes again.

Acting? For me that was the final curtain.

Harold Forwell, Leicester

SOOTY SINGING SHOCK

You have to admire the determination of performers to cash in on their TV exposure by doing Christmas pantomimes.

We went to see Wayne Sleep as Simple Simon in Jack and the Beanstalk at the Theatre Royal, Windsor.

I felt it was a shame that such a talented dancer should be reduced to blundering about alongside Dora Bryan's Fairy.

She seemed out of place not walking into a bath with a door on the side of it. But biggest contrivance of the lot was the Sooty puppet. He may be sweet on TV but what are his credentials for theatre work? He can't walk, he can't dance and he can't sing. He can't even speak.

Yet this tiny orange glove puppet character was passed off as a star of the show.

Morris Daventree, Slough

THE PANTOMIME THAT NEVER WAS

Why have one of those tired old shows that everyone has seen before when you can have your very own pantomime dreamt up by creative people in your very own village?

The committee at Merton in Devon were sold the idea of something different by Bob Harrod.

He worked up a script that was full of new jokes, and addressed some contemporary issues in the county and farther afield.

But the committee started to get cold feet when they saw the title of Bob's script: Snow White and the Seven Asylum Seekers.

Em, were they drifting into problematic territory here?

You bet.

A volunteer read through the pages of the Harrod text and decided there were parts that wouldn't go down well with the Commission for Racial Equality.

So Bob was asked to do some re-writes.

But no writer likes being told to change his words by some committee.

Naturally Bob refused. They had to go with what he'd done or he'd withdraw his whole script.

(Well, he was only following in the footsteps of Samuel Becket and Harold Pinter. And, let's face it, how many great pantomimes have they got to their names?)

But the committee was not going to be dictated to by an arty type. Oh, no, that's not how things work in deepest Devon.

So the show was stopped in its tracks.

And everyone took the huff.

But by the following summer they had all kissed and made up, and Bob returned to his word processor.

This time he came up with an endearing proposition: "Snow Person and the Seven Completely Ordinary People". Now who could take offence to that?

BUM ACT
We took our grandchildren to see Cinderella at the Grand Theatre, Wolverhampton. We were all enjoying it until one of the Grumbleweeds roller-skated across the stage apparently completely naked.
It was a horrible sight which I couldn't get out of my head right over Christmas.

Christine Graham, Staffordshire

WHERE'S THE VIDEO?
After years of chuckling at the misfortunes of others, as the hostess of 'You've been framed' (the family-falling-over TV clips show), Lisa Reilly became a victim of an accident herself. Between performances of Cinderella at the Regent Theatre, Stoke-on-Trent, the big girl toppled down some stairs and broke a couple of her toes, forcing her to limp back on stage in a big pair of slippers.
Unfortunately no-one captured the fall on tape, because, of course, they could have sold it to TV producers.

HE'S IN FRONT OF YOU.
I played the part of Cinderella in our local am dram Christmas show. I'm not a great singer, but I can just about hold a song.

I had this one nerve-wracking number at the start of Act Two after I've returned from the ball.

The audience had only just settled down before I launched into it. But one night I had competition. A man in the audience started howling. Not with laughter, but in pain.

There was a dreadful commotion in the middle of the auditorium. At first I thought I'd persevere, but the distractions were too much for me.

The man collapsed and died of a heart attack.

We abandoned the show for that evening, and on the next night I didn't attempt the song. The whole event had shattered my somewhat shaky self-confidence.

Phyllis McDonald, Grampian

STAGE CRAFT

As drama students in Nottingham we were appallingly pretentious; snottily dismissive of aspects of what I now appreciate were marvellous, intelligent productions mounted by the Nottingham Playhouse.

When one of our number got himself a minor part in the Theatre Royal's pantomime, we were scathing of his sell out to commercialism.

Andy had been signed up as an assistant stage manager, and then the director decided to give him a brief on-stage role as the Mayor with a few lines delivered to Mike and Bernie Winters.

Andy's peers, including me, did everything we could to make our fellow drama student feel dreadful about his demeaning undertaking but, to his credit, he just got on with it.

The rest of us decided to go and see him in the show, and met for a few drinks beforehand.

We were well oiled before taking our seats in the Gods. We were giggling and generally being a nuisance even before the curtain went up. As the company sang and danced their way through the first big number we started yelling: "We want the Mayor." When Andy appeared for the first time we roared our approval, and chanted "And-ee, And-ee, And-ee," drowning out his dialogue, and that of the Winters brothers, who looked disapprovingly up to the top deck of the theatre, along with most of the audience.

As soon as Andy left the stage, we booed loudly and then started our chant for "Bring back Andy."

To his credit, Bernie Winters had a damned good stab at silencing us troublesome hecklers and got rounds of applause from the audience who were understandably immensely irritated at our childish behaviour.

The theatre manager and some ushers arrived at our seats and demanded we leave, which we did.

And unfortunately Andy was sacked from the show at the end of that evening. Shame on us for ruining his debut.

Like the rest of us, he didn't make it in the acting profession, but at least he could say he'd shared the stage with a couple of Britain's top comedians.

Vincent Thorgood, Edinburgh

HOW HAVE YOU BEAN?

Jack and the Beanstalk was made for the Krankies, and vice versa.

You remember the Krankies – the Scots bloke with the little kid being a nuisance beside him all the time – wee Jimmy Krankie (who is actually a woman, Janette Tough; and not just any woman but in real life the wife of the stooge one, Ian Tough).

Well, think about it. You need a Jack. Look no farther than Wee Jimmy.

And you need a Jack's mother, who gives the boy a cow to take to market.

That's got to be the other Krankie in drag, hasn't it?

Great. Two key members of the cast signed up in a single deal.

Plus a string of economies of scale: one dressing room for the pair of them, one hotel room between them. One taxi to get them back at night.

Mm, a pantomime accountant's dream.

Okay, so they don't get as much TV exposure as they used to, but no worries – come December and January, the duo are in demand.

Last year the good people of Glasgow were lucky to have the talented team come to town – at the Pavilion Theatre for a short season.

But the season was shorter than it should have been – because of the beanstalk – that didn't do what stalks are supposed to.

The show featured a rather fancy mechanical device. A new improvement to the traditional expanding cardboard stalk. This one was designed to miraculously rise beyond the proscenium arch, with Jack holding on to it.

Em, good plan. But as we know with panto, not everything always goes to plan, and at the end of an Act One matinee, as the curtain came down with Jack high up the stalk, the stalk and Jack came down, unplanned.

Yes, Janette crashed on to the stage.

In the interval the kids had all the time in the world to eat ice cream, the Dads could queue for a second pint, because there was no Second Act that day.

Poor Janette was rushed to the nearest A&E.

Next day substitutes were deployed in the roles of Jack and the Widow, and some people told the local papers that it just wasn't the same, and they wanted their money back.

Well, naturally, because there can be no satisfactory substitute for the Krankies in this show.

In July, their manager told us the unfortunate event and its repercussions were still being investigated.

"We demand more money! We're not carol singers, we're pop idols."

ROLL ON NEXT YEAR

On New Year's Eve 30 million people drink 18 million gallons of booze, which will cause one-in-ten to throw up.

1.2 million people will get involved in a scuffle.

800,000 will meet their future marriage partner (or perhaps we should say: one of their future marriage partners).

140,000 babies will be conceived.

And 60,000 people will be arrested.

There's patently a connection between these statistics, but we'll leave that for you to figure out.

BAD VIEW

The year end edition of the Economist magazine was designed to get people in a mood.

For what is hard to say.

The text around the cover photograph of Planet Earth from space said: "The end of the world".

MEANT TO BE FUNNY

The Daily Mail's film critic Christopher Tookey gave his top turkey award of 2004 to 'Sex Lives of Potato Men': *"The most witless, inept and repulsive British comedy I have ever had the misfortune to see."*

LOOKING BAD

One regional newspaper gave End-of-Year Awards for memorable contributions to fashion.

The columnists reckoned Charlotte Church had achieved the most stunning transformation from child with the voice of an angel to fully rounded beautiful woman.

They perhaps saw fit to turn a blind eye to the bottom end of the tabloids where the beautiful woman could sometimes be seen staggering in the gutter after a session of heavy drinking in the big city.

But other commentators declared this quality was Charlotte's greatest strength – successful singer doesn't slope off to snooty inaccessible lifestyle, but just gets on with what lots of young women like doing on a Saturday night – except in her case she can't go far without reptilian photographers aiming their long lens at her.

Good on you, Charlotte.

ANY LAST WORDS?

Most bitter business quote of 2004 came from the foul Italian mouth of the expelled financial director of Parmalat, speaking to journalists trying to interview him on his doorstep: *"I wish you and your families a slow and painful death."*

SEE OUT THE OLD

20% of sudden deaths from heart malfunction may be due to emotional stress, reported the London University Centre for Cardiology in their Brain magazine. This encouraged one regional newspaper to come up with the headline: *'Excitement of New Year may end up killing you'.*

FINE FOOTWORK

A restaurant in Cambridge advertised a New Year's Eve event consisting of a meal followed by a disco, but the council spotted the restaurant did not have the appropriate licence and so advised the owners that if dancing took place on the premises they might face a £5,000 fine.

NEIGHBOURLY

There's a degree of tension in our cul de sac throughout the year, but the atmosphere always gets worse in the month of December.

Essentially there are two groupings of people and they don't get on with each other. Around Christmas there are little drinks parties, and, to the embarrassment of everyone, two separate patterns of visits operate, and there's little overlap between the two.

Everyone exchanges Christmas cards, but one half of the cards include an invitation to a friend's soiree, and the other half don't.

It's been going on like this for years, and you certainly could not describe it as the season of goodwill to all mankind. It's like two parallel universes of goodwill to half mankind.

Two years ago a new couple moved into one of the houses in the autumn, and by Christmas they had still not fallen into one camp or the other, so they invited all the people in the Close to a New Year's Eve party.

Most people went along, probably, like us, in the hope that this would for once and for all break down the barrier of the cul de sac of two halves. But it didn't. The separate groupings quickly formed in the house, one lot in the front room, the rest in the kitchen.

Even the midnight chimes on TV didn't trigger a round of best wishes across the opposing camps.

Everyone went home having only wished Happy New Year to those from their own tribe.

The newcomers couldn't stand it and they put their house up for sale in March.

Donna Forsyth, Surrey

SMILE, PLEASE

You go to Rome to see in the New Year in style – amidst thousands of revellers in the Piazza Navona Square.

You've got a camera with a nice, neat tripod, so you won't end up with fuzzy snaps. It's all going exceedingly well until you spot a group of well-wishers fussing round some smart-looking bloke in a suit.

Not wanting to miss out, you take a few steps in the direction of the crowd.

Blow me, it's the country's Prime Minister, that bastard Berlusconi.

For years you've hated his guts. And now he's here - right in front of you. Why, if you got yourself in a good position, you could shake his hand.

But you'd prefer to wring his neck, however in a crowded square on New Year's Eve is not the place for that.

So next best thing – throw your tripod at him (you'd always been good at the javelin).

And it's a hit. Got him in the back of his greasy head.

Okay, you're arrested and kept in a cell for the night, but more than one observer congratulated you on your impromptu effort to bring the billionaire businessman and modern Machiavelli down a peg or two.

WHO ORDERED BEANS ON TOAST?

How can you get away from the great unwashed on New Year's Eve? Easy. Just book a table at the Cipriani restaurant in Mayfair. A slap-up seven course supper and all the booze you can pour down your neck for just £650 per head. Oh, and if you're still thinking you might be surrounded by riff-raff, then you can pay a bit more to get into the private dining room at the back. This is where Elton John comes to get away from cheapskate autograph hunters, who would doubtless pester him in the kebab queue.

MAKING A RESOLUTION?

Only 54% of New Year Resolutions survive for more than seven days. So this year, resolve to do better.

WHAT A FAG

My New Year's Resolution was to give up smoking.
It didn't start well because I meant to have my last cigarette before the chimes of midnight and I forgot, so I had my last one at about quarter past twelve.
I got up in the morning determined to start a new cigarette-free life.
It lasted until eleven o'clock.

Billy Freeman, Middlesbrough

CHANGING BEHAVIOUR

The Sunday Mirror's Sex Doctor, Catherine Hood, offered readers ten New Year recommendations, including watching porn films, dressing as a fireman, learning stripping techniques, having sex out of doors and making your own home sex video.

DAY TO LOOK FORWARD TO

Come the end of Christmas Eve, you're just a month away from things looking up.

Cardiff University social scientists analysed the graph of down-heartedness that follows Christmas and concluded that the lowest point is reached on the 24th January. This is when the cheerfulness of Christmas has completely disappeared, the New Year's Resolutions have gone out the window, the weather's delivered its maximum miserableness, and the credit card statements for your pre-Christmas excess have turned up.

Then, as from the 25th of January, apparently things don't seem quite so bad.

MIRACLE BARGAIN

It's a pity Jesus wasn't born in January. I could have bought all my presents in the Sales, and saved myself a packet.

Mervyn Hancock, Western Daily Press

PITY THE POOR BANKER

Spare a thought for all those people who work in banks or insurance offices. Yes, we see them looking glum through most of the year, but apparently in January their hearts sink to an even deeper low.

According to research, almost 50% of financial service workers seriously contemplate tendering their resignations in the first month of the New Year.

BRIEF RETIREMENT

An annuity firm offered enhanced pensions for certain New Year customers - those people over 65 who smoke, have high blood pressure, excess cholesterol, are over-weight or suffer insulin-dependent diabetes.

According to the actuaries, it works out cheaper for them in the long run, if you see what they mean.

CHILLING PROSPECT

When should the season of goodwill commence?

Not until the 1st of December say Norwegian Future-in-our-Hands campaigners. They tried to persuade Oslo Council to ban the marketing of Christmas goods in the shops until that date.

To show they meant it, five of them dressed up as Santas and threw themselves into the city harbour in September when the water temperature was just 4 Centigrade.

May have achieved a brief freeze on something.

PLANS FOR NEXT YEAR?

Don't bother - apart from praying a lot - reckon an obscure south-east Asian religious cult.

They are convinced the world will end in 2006.

"Don't you love it! When Christmas is over and the days start to get longer!"

OOPS

A&E departments analysed the causes of Christmas accidents and discovered that stairs and steps were the most dangerous thing at Christmas. 7,500 people took a trip to hospital as a result of a mishap down steps.

But the second biggest source of seasonal disasters lay in bed. Yes, 2,800 people claimed their tragedy happened between the sheets, or getting out of bed. How? We wish we knew.

Third was the Christmas tree – of course – damn, dangerous things.

Fourth: kitchen knives. What – are they sharp or something and no-one realised?

Five was the drinking glass. What are these people up to? Don't they drink during the rest of the year? Why can't they cope with a glass at Christmas? Well, 600 couldn't, and had to go into hospital to have bits of broken glass removed from some part of their anatomy, and the gashes they'd made in themselves stitched up.

At Number Six, the TV. How come this box in the corner of the living room suddenly rises up to terrify the household during the holidays? Surely not all the 230 cases were of people putting their foot through the screen in despair at the specials?

Finally – because we can go no further – at seventh position, with 185 victims of its vicious behaviour, inexplicable cruelty and violent tendencies, rang in the telephone.

Yes, the telephone was the cause of nearly two hundred people seeking emergency attention from the medics.

Doh, no, we just don't get it either.

Here are a few more horrors…

TIME RUNNING OUT

You think of Rolex watches, you think of a quality timepiece - not radioactivity. But back in 1959, when no-one knew better, the Swiss watch firm stuck strontium 90 in some of their up-market items.

Once it had been figured out that this wasn't a healthy proposition, the American atomic energy authority was given the task of tracking down the offending Christmas gifts.

Fairly easy job.

They just had to walk down New York streets with a Geiger counter.

THE LAST NOEL

A tradition on our estate was to go round carol singing and in the process raise money for a good cause. We'd meet at the church hall and have a fortifying sherry before we began. Usually it would turn out to be quite a boozy night as a number of homes would invite us in for a drink. In fact, the danger was drinking too much as the evening wore on.

One year I certainly had more than I should have. The carol singing party got a bit straggly as a result of our intoxication. We were giggling our way along in the dark between houses.

One front drive had a big hole in it where work was being done on the drains. Somehow I went through the barriers instead of going round and fell down into the hole.

Strangely I did this silently, and didn't shout out to the others ahead of me. They knocked on the front door and were invited into the house. The door closed, and I was left on my own to clamber out of the hole. I felt really stupid and was covered in mud, so I went home.

And guess what? My so-called friends didn't even miss me. None of them came to find me, or phoned later to check I was all right.

Sally Waine, Newcastle-under-Lyme

IT'S AGONY, AUNT

We were astounded at some of the subject matter which desperate people brought to the attention of the advice experts of the popular newspapers.

The Sun's Deirdre Sanders must get more letters than Santa at this time of year.

Here are a few snippets she kindly let us sample from her postbag:

I promised my son that Santa would make up for him having no presents last year, but there's no chance because two weeks ago my ex. stole £350 I'd saved up for presents, outings and a school uniform.

I've had sex with my boyfriend's mate and now I don't know which one to choose.

My oldest daughter has invited the whole family for Christmas Day, except for one sister she doesn't talk to. It's breaking my heart.

I've been having sex with my mother-in-law, Now she's blackmailing me into buying her expensive gifts.

My girlfriend brought home perfume, jewellery and flowers at Christmas saying they were presents from female workmates. I'm frantic with worry they may have been from men.

I asked my girlfriend what she wanted for Christmas and she said a sex toy. I was horrified. My manhood is very small and now I feel more inadequate than ever.

Mercifully, Deirdre had a helpful answer to every one of these, em, seasonal love stories.

MASS HYSTERIA

The Christmas (2004) edition of 'The Vicar of Dibley' was staggeringly distasteful. The first half featured most characters describing their sexual fantasies, that, for one, included a lesbian affair with the Queen. Then we got the reading aloud of proposed hymn verses, each one offering up more offensive Christian analogies than the last. I can't bring myself to repeat them. Finally we saw Dawn French drunk in the pulpit at Midnight Mass unable to remember the name of the baby whose birth she was supposed to be leading prayers for. Does no-one in the hierarchy see fit to evaluate this material before it's put together? Are they all too smug in the belief they are geniuses? I noticed they ran the repeat on a Saturday night in August – thus doubtless fulfilling contracts and spreading the cost of this ill-conceived investment, and perhaps acknowledging they had delivered an absolute stinker that soured Christmas Day for many a family.

Angie Duncan, London

HOME ALONE

I've always been wary of home delivery supermarket shopping but I thought it might be the answer just before Christmas.

I placed my order via the internet and the acknowledgement advised that it would be delivered on Christmas Eve. So I stayed in all day. I rang the supermarket twice asking for a rough time of arrival. They said between 2.30 and 4.30. At twenty past five their van turned up and I took possession of the bags from a young man who looked like he'd had a drink.

He was very keen to dump my bags and head off. But I insisted he stay until I'd checked the contents, which proved to be completely wrong. He'd obviously dropped my shopping off somewhere else.

He offered to go and find it, but I decided it was too late in the day for that, so I said I'd hang on to what he'd delivered.

I had to make up my Christmas day meals from someone else's shopping, and someone else presumably had to do the same from my order.

Never again.

Dorothy Wilton, Hounslow

BLESS HER

Even Her Majesty - having devoted the whole of her life to honourable public service - is unable to stay within a trouble-free bubble at this time of year.

On Christmas Day 2004 she stood up from the dining table, and so a footman moved her chair away.

What's a footman?

A personal flunkie who pours the gravy for you, and the sherry (Therein may lie a clue).

Gosh, that's handy. Can we get one of those at Tescos?

No. And seconds later the Queen went to sit down again, and the chair had gone, so she stumbled backwards on to a couple of corgis (not toy cars) and ended up on the Sandringham carpet.

FOLLOW THE DRILL

My Dad got a Black and Decker electric drill for Christmas from my Mum. Because of the weight of the box, he knew what it was before he'd unwrapped it. It was her way of trying to encourage him to do some jobs around the house – which he hated doing.

As soon as he'd got the drill out of the box, Mum started pointing out things he could usefully do with it.

As the day went on we all came up with more and more elaborate suggestions of what he could achieve on the DIY front now that he had this marvellous tool – make a shelf unit, knock a new door through to the kitchen, erect an extension. The ribbing went on alongside the drinking. Then my little brother said we could use it to clean our ears by putting a cotton bud in the drill instead of one of the metal bits.

Dad was drunk by now and he went and got a cotton bud and fixed it into the drill.

We were all laughing at the sight of the cotton bud spinning round on the end of the big electrical machine. Then Dad stuck it against his ear for a second, and said it was a lovely sensation.

A few seconds later he lifted it up to his ear again, but this time pushed it too far. His face suddenly went white and he switched the drill off and carefully put it down.

Blood was coming out of his ear.

He'd torn the side of his ear canal.

We called an ambulance and got him to hospital. He was kept in for two days. He's lost some of his hearing in that ear, but Mum never asks him to do jobs around the house any more.

Michael Roberon, St. Albans

BEST FOOT FORWARD

We are all made well aware of the dangers of drinking and driving, but Alcohol Concern was at pains to point out that drinking and walking is more likely to lead to a fatality.

Twice as many drunken pedestrians are killed in road accidents in the weeks before Christmas than drivers.

STILL FREAKS ME OUT

I was having a fling with an attractive woman whose relationship with her husband had gone very sour. And that suited me, because I was in a similar state with my wife.

We used to meet at bars and hotels and, occasionally, when we were confident the coast was clear, at each other's homes.

We knew seeing each other over Christmas wasn't going to be possible, then Margie saw that The Giveheads, a band her husband raved about, were playing a gig not far away on Christmas Eve. So she got three tickets, one for husband Malcolm, and one each for their two kids, so they could go, leaving her to get on with preparing stuff for Christmas Day.

Great scheme.

Meanwhile I told my wife I was going down the pub with my mates from work. Margie told me to come round after 8 o'clock. I was really chuffed at this chance for us to make love on Christmas Eve. This was going to be my Christmas prezzie all right.

Margie was dressed up very sexy when I got there.

I'd brought a bottle of cold white wine from the offie. We agree that I would leave at 9.30 pm to be on the safe side. Not wanting to waste our time we went straight to bed.

We had just started to make love when Margie suddenly went rigid. She'd heard a car pull up on the drive.

We leapt out of bed and she looked out the window, and, yes, Malcolm and the kids were back.

She ran to the landing and pulled down the flap to get into the attic. It had one of those built-in ladders, and I was up it with my clothes in my hands like a rocket.

I could hear the front door opening and there wasn't time for Margie to shut the flap without Malcolm being aware of it, so she left it open.

She'd darted back into the bedroom to tidy up.

The band had cancelled the gig and Malcolm had decided to come back.

Their attic didn't seem to have any flooring in and so I had to balance on the rafters. Part of me was glad Margie hadn't closed the flap as I could get my bearings with the bit of light. But I was sure Malcolm would be able to hear my heart beating.

I was frantic.

I could see Margie had got her clothes on. She went downstairs, leaving me balanced precariously on the rafters.

What on earth was I to do? How could I possibly get out without Malcolm finding out?

I could hear Margie trying to get on with things as if everything was perfectly normal. I was afraid to move a muscle as it might make a noise that would bring Malcolm up in my direction.

I assumed that Margie would try to get them all in the kitchen to give me a chance to get down the ladder and out of the house, but they didn't settle. They were all drifting around from room to room.

Margie came up the stairs and looked up into the attic but didn't dare speak.

Next minute Malcolm came up the stairs and asked her why the attic flap was open. She told him she'd been keeping her Christmas presents up there. He said: "Oh, it must be a big one then."

He started to close the flap, but the folding ladder caught on one of my shoes and so it stuck part open. He tried a couple of times and I was frozen in fear, wondering what I should do.

Margie decided to distract him and started to seduce him. He abandoned the folding ladder in a half closed position and responded to her advances, and the next minute they were off into their bedroom where Margie and I had been just half an hour previously.

I saw this as my chance to escape but I couldn't move the ladder from the inside without making a hell of a racket. Just touching it rattled the aluminium, so I was trapped.

I could hear them making love.

After a while they were up and about again.

I kept thinking Margie would get everyone out of the way, but it didn't happen. As I waited I tried to reposition myself across the rafters to get more comfortable, but every way I squatted was painful and I kept getting cramps or pins and needles.

After an hour or so they all went to bed, leaving me in the pitch dark.

I then assumed her plan was that once they were all fast asleep she would come and extract me. But that didn't happen either.

I wanted to shout out: "For God's sake, get me out of here!"

I was desperate for a pee. I could feel there was some stuff in a cardboard box. There was something in a plastic bag, so I carefully removed the object inside which felt like a camera, and I relieved myself in the bag. This made a heck of a noise and I was amazed Malcolm didn't get up and discover me.

I tried opening the flap again but the noise was terrible. So I took the most tolerable position across the rafters I could achieve and waited for Margie to rescue me.

As you can imagine, it was the longest night of my life.

About four in the morning I got terrible stomach cramps. I desperately needed the toilet.

I was forced to take everything out of the cardboard box and use the box as a toilet.

I drifted off to sleep for a few minutes after that, then woke thinking this had all just been a nightmare, but I realised it wasn't. It was true. I was living a nightmare.

I was also now thinking what on earth would my wife be thinking. She would have chased up my mates who would have told her I never came near the pub that night. She might have been on to the police and the hospital trying to track me down.

Part of me wanted to come clean with Malcolm and apologise to him and get out of the house and go home and try to mend things there. But I reckoned it wasn't fair on Malcolm and the kids to spoil their Christmas Day by suddenly appearing out of the attic.

Before dawn I could hear Margie's children wake up and start to unwrap their presents. I was like a spy on another family's Christmas morning, whilst I was absent without leave from my own home where my wife and daughter were probably witless with worry as to where I'd disappeared to.

I now assumed Margie would get them all out of the house for a walk or something so I could make my escape. But it didn't happen.

I was thirsty and hungry and aching all over and I now contemplated spending the whole of Christmas Day in this cell at the top of their house.

I placed a foot on each of two rafters and tried to do exercises to get my circulation going.

I could hear Margie talking about cooking the turkey. I couldn't believe she could abandon me for so long. Was she punishing me for having created this mess for her? Had she forgotten I was up here? All sorts of terrible thoughts passed through my head. I even toyed with trying to make a hole in the roof to climb through and jump down into the garden. The trouble was my every movement seemed to make a huge noise and the whole of the attic was like an echo chamber.

Suddenly all of these problems became insignificant.

The door bell rang. It was my wife, Angela. She wanted to know where I was. She told Malcolm she had found out I had been having an affair with his wife. At first Margie denied this. Angela said she was sure I'd been round here last night and that I hadn't come home.

Malcolm suddenly stomped up the stairs and opened the flap and lowered the loft ladder. I didn't wait for him to come up to find me. I started to climb down. He got hold of my foot and wrenched it off the ladder causing me to fall down the front of the ladder, which knocked out several of my teeth. He kicked me in the groin whilst I was on the floor. I picked myself up and tried to apologise. He and Angela were both screaming at me.

I got down the stairs and out the front door. A friend of Angela's was in a car outside. I didn't get in. Angela slapped and punched me, then got in the car and they drove away.

I walked to the end of the road. I saw no point in going home that day and so I walked to a Travelodge on the ring road and checked in there.

I never spent another night in my own home.

Angela and I were divorced six months later.

Margie stayed with Malcolm and her kids. We didn't see each other any more. It turned out she thought I had escaped when she had gone to bed to make love to Malcolm. She was amazed I'd spent all night at her house.

On Christmas afternoon Malcolm went into the attic and discovered that I'd used the cardboard box as a toilet.

He took the box and its contents, and the plastic bag of urine round to our house and banged on the door, all set to beat me up. Angela told him she didn't know where I was, which was the truth.

He hurled the box at our living room window, yelled his head off and walked away, I was told.

As I sat in the lonely comfort of the motel, I kept thinking about how and when the mess I'd left in the attic would be discovered.

I bet no-one's got a worst story than this for your book.

I'm glad I've written it down. And I hereby apologise again to Malcolm, Angela, Margie and the children for all the trouble I caused.

Richard, London

ACKNOWLEDGMENTS

The author and publishers are very grateful to all the people who offered us information for this book.

To the best of our knowledge the tales are true, though some have been disguised to take the pain out of it for the victims.

People responded to our advertising and press coverage and so offered us their stories and experiences of seasonal difficulties. We have also contacted individuals or journalists as a result of seeing articles in various publications.

Our thanks to the editorial personnel at the national and regional newspapers who kindly agreed to us quoting their headlines and copy in order that we could review and critique the spirit and letter of Christmas as presented on their pages. Many busy staffers also helped us contact the sources of their stories, for which we are most appreciative.

We are indebted to everyone who was happy to expose their unhappy experiences within these pages, or to allow us to make use of the recollections of others. Thanks specifically to June Ehrlich for permitting us to draw from her book about her husband's war time experiences, 'His Silver Wings', in our Good Old Days chapter.

We sincerely trust we have accurately reflected the information provided.
If anything is incorrect, we apologise.

We much appreciate all the advice we have received from the compliance lawyers at Cobbetts in Birmingham, and from Jonathan Holder.

Where possible we have sought verification, clarification and clearance to make reference to other people's descriptions and information. If there are any instances wherein our efforts have failed to satisfactorily confirm elements of the material, or permissions to make reference to that material, we apologise, and hereby offer to provide redress in our next year's book, if it proceeds to publication.

In some instances we have been asked to change names and locations to protect anonymity, and in some cases we have counselled against using real names and locations.

We believe we have got this right. If not, once again, apologies.

ANOTHER BAD CHRISTMAS

HAVE YOU GOT A GOOD STORY?

Maybe we're mad, but we may do this again next year.

We had lots of good stories for which we didn't have enough space to use.

(Please don't harass us by demanding to know why we used someone else's and not yours. It's about balance, essentially.)

But we might try and do the same next year, so if you've got a Christmas story that would amuse others to know about, please send us the details.

And if we think there is a worthwhile vein of journalism and publishing here, then we might tackle some other subjects.

The ones we currently have short-listed are:

BAD GIGS - the boys and girls in and around the band have a terrible time.

BAD NEIGHBOURS - Get off your chest the pain of those awful people.

BAD HOLIDAYS - horror stories when you tried to take a break.

BAD SHOPPING - the customer's frequently wrong.

BAD WORK - terrible experiences from the world of employment.

MAD MEDIA - workers in, or victims of, newspaper and broadcasting lunacy.

WEB WEIRDOS - your nasty nightmares from the internet.

Send your stories to;
Severnpix, P.O. Box 468, Worcester, WR6 5ZR.
Or e-mail to severnpix@tiscali.co.uk.

THE GUILTY PARTIES

MIKE JACKSON
Worked in the television industry for 25 years as a writer, producer and director.
He produced ITV children's presentation and promotion in the 1980s at Central TV in Birmingham, then became a freelance location director for lots of popular BBC programmes from 'The Antiques Roadshow' to 'Music Live'.
He's written comic fringe theatre plays and has scripted hundreds of humorous definitions for the star guests of 'Call my Bluff'.
He devised and co-wrote the ITV children's comedy serial 'Minty', shot in Australia and screened all over the world.
And Mike's written three popular books about British motorways in the last three years: The M4, M5 and M6 Sights Guides.

ADEY BRYANT
A Portsmouth boy, Adey accumulated 300 rejection slips before The Sun first published one of his cartoons 25 years ago. Since then his work and humour have been enjoyed in Punch, Private Eye, The Daily Mirror, The Spectator, The Insider, and in many women's magazines and some men's magazines. He's done coal-face work on Christmas cards in his time, which has helped him meet the sundry financial commitments he has acquired over the years as a result of his various happy marriages. He now lives under a rock in the Fens with his eleventh wife Kim.

LISA GRIFFITHS
Young, attractive, dynamic, talented and hard-working with two small kids and one big garden to look after. Hard to believe she's been a print designer in the Midlands for many years with hundreds of specialist brochures, advertising campaigns and books under her belt.